NUTRITIONIST IN PRIVATE PRACTICE

Lessons Learned from My First Year in Business

AMY HAGER, RDN, CDE

Table of Contents

Foreword

As nutrition professionals working in the trenches, we are privy to a unique vantage point. We often witness both sides of the health and wellness equation. On one hand, we see the debilitating impact of the obesity crisis, uncontrolled diabetes, heart disease, cancer, autoimmune disorders, the rise of chronic disease and resulting human suffering. The statistics can be quite sobering. Thankfully, we also know what's possible. We are charged with the awesome privilege and responsibility of being agents of change, acting as the necessary conduit by partnering with our clients, supporting them in their quest for improved health through sustainable lifestyle change. It's the transformations that we get to see, with our clients, that make our job incredibly fulfilling.

When I met Amy back in 2011, during an intensive year long advanced coach training program, I knew I had stumbled upon that rare person who had the fortitude, creativity and trust in herself to follow the path of her own entrepreneurial dreams, wherever they may lead. At the time we were deeply entrenched in honing our own skills as transformational coaches within our respective fields; Amy was working in the corporate sector as a nutrition and wellness coach and I was busy finishing an MBA, running my nutrition therapy and coaching practice, and was laying the groundwork for my eventual transition into business coaching for nutrition and wellness professionals. We connected on our shared a passion for all things nutrition, coaching and especially the notion that we really can forge our own destinies by being true to ourselves. Not long after we finished our training, I was delighted to get a call from Amy to chat about her plans to start her own practice, which eventually lead us down the path of creating several collaborative opportunities, as described in her book.

Let me say upfront, that you are in for a treat. Amy's book is a gift to anyone with even an inkling to step into the entrepreneurial world of private practice. In it, she generously shares her journey transitioning from a regular paycheck and relatively predictable environment as a corporate nutrition coach to her new role, as a full-time creative entrepreneur and private practice nutritionist. You won't find MBA-like jargon, nor does it necessarily follow a "how to" type of format focusing on the mechanics of starting and operating a practice. Instead, Amy astutely recognized a void in the current book market and filled it by serving up something much more unique, timely and valuable: an honest and detailed portrayal of her twelve-month adventure with all of the ups and downs along the way. Each chapter will walk you through a variety of decision points, how she evaluated her options, and how she knew she was moving in the right direction with her business. Particularly notable is Amy's candor in describing the process by which she built her practice with insurance based clients and her experiences in becoming credentialed through various plans and how she went about

setting specific income goals and the strategies she imple-
mented to meet them. Each vignette provides a valuable
snapshot of what's possible for nutritionists who yearn to
blaze their own trail in private practice.

As I was preparing to write the foreword for Amy's book,
I found myself perusing through some of the employment
projections and growth statistics for the field of dietetics
and nutrition. Intuitively, we know that the need for our
services is profound and clearly on the upswing and the
outcomes we provide are measurable. What I didn't realize is just how much growth is actually expected. The
US Bureau of Labor and Statistics predicts that the employment of dietitians and nutritionists will increase 20%
from 2010 to 2020; that's 6% faster than the average 14%
growth of all occupations. In the coming years, demand
for our services will further be spurred by the growing and
aging population and one that is wanting a more personalized approach to nutrition care. Wow! This presents an
incredible opportunity for nutritionists, and I believe that it
beautifully sets the stage for those with a flair for entrepreneurial ventures.

Gone are the days when you graduated from your nutrition program or internship only to discover that the only
viable options for making a living in your chosen field was
pretty limited; to getting a job as a clinical dietitian in a
hospital setting, a government subsidized outpatient clinic
or in a food service setting. Now, the possibilities are almost limitless and will continue to morph and grow in the
future with all indicators pointing front and center to private

practice being a wonderful option for those who chose the self-employed path.

As a business coach to wellness professionals, I witness firsthand, the passion and commitment that nutritionists bring to their profession. Most come up the path with extensive training in a variety of specialty areas and clinical settings. Anyone who dreams of moving into the world of entrepreneurism is likely attracted to the sense of freedom, flexibility, unlimited income potential and the ability to work with clients in a way that is most efficient and effective. Many would like to start their own practice but aren't sure how to manage all the moving parts or where to begin in the process in getting clients. Often times dietitians and nutritionists struggle with the misguided illusion that what's lacking is more clinical training or another certification before they'll finally be ready to take the courageous plunge into private practice. While continued education IS important, often the chronic pursuit of more training turns out to be a way of postponing the discomfort of the unknown.

Starting your own private practice will be a bit scary at times. But it will likely be the one of the most rewarding decisions you'll make in your life and career. My deepest sentiment is to encourage each of you to to take action, use what you know today, and begin the process of crafting your own destiny.

Lesli Koskela, MBA, RDN, LDN
Business Coach & Mentor
www.leslikoskela.com

About the Author

A my Hager has been a Registered Dietitian Nutritionist since 2004. She received her Bachelor's Degree in Dietetics from the University of Vermont and her Master's Degree in Nutrition from Meredith College. She is trained as a Health and Wellness Coach through Wellcoaches and holds an advanced certification from the institution. She is also a Certified Diabetes Educator and helps facilitate group education to patients dealing with the disease. She currently works in private practice in Greensboro, North Carolina.

When not advising clients on healthy eating, she spends her time engrossed in a variety of hobbies. She is passionate about beekeeping, and has kept bees for the past 4 years in her urban backyard. She also embraces her creative side by designing jewelry and organic skin-care products. She has an Etsy shop, Bee Happy Life, where her bee inspired creations have been delighting others around the globe since 2013. Additionally, she enjoys participating in local craft shows and festivals to share her craftsmanship. She's authored a book on called "The Crafty Beekeeper," which is available as a Kindle book on Amazon.

Recently, Amy has been focused on helping others achieve goals similar to hers. She advises other nutritionists and students on the art of self employment and private practice through her Mentoring services. She is also dedicated to helping others craft the lifestyles of their dreams in her Life Crafting Coaching services. She believes that we are all capable and deserving to live meaningful and purposeful lives through intentional design. She uses a creative approach to help others become artisans in creating their ideal lifestyle.

Amy can be found online at:

website: www.BeeHappyLife.com

Instagram: @beehappylife

Pinterest: www.pinterest.com/beehappylife

Facebook: www.facebook.com/beehappylife

Twitter: @beehappylife

A Note from the Author

When I was toying with the idea of starting my own nutrition business there were so many thoughts racing through my mind. The logistics of how to actually execute the idea was at the top of the list. But what really had me curious was the experience of it all. What was it actually like to start a business? What was the transition like leaving the corporate world, going into business for yourself? I wanted to know and was dying to find out the personal story behind being a nutritionist in private practice.

When I was in school and doing my dietetic internship, I learned that one of my instructors had her own business. This was completely novel to me. Every single one of the rotations during my internship featured dietitians working in different settings, but none who were self employed. It seemed like a mystery. How did she get clients? How did she collect payment? How did she keep her business running steady? I found out that in addition to her business she also taught classes, was an advisory spokesperson for the Pork Council, in addition to wearing other hats. It seemed so intriguing, so interesting to do work that has so much variety and completely opposite from the 9 to 5 work week.

The idea of self employment stayed in the back of my head, or perhaps more precisely, in the center of my heart for many years. Although I had the good fortune to start out my career with job positions that had more variety and appeal than working in a clinical setting. Working in a wellness center, or in diabetes education and eventually health coaching I had lots of opportunity for creativity and flexibility in my role as a dietitian. As I grew tired or bored of one position, I would "trade up" and look for the next new, exciting challenge. But eventually the same discontent would reappear after a few years in a new role and I knew it was time to address the underlying issue, that I wanted to work for myself.

I knew that private practice was not only possible but that many many dietitians were doing it successfully. So where to jump in? Where to start? Who to talk to? In my 4 year dietetic nutrition program there was no course that oriented young, engaged nutritionists-to-be on how to start a business. It's been suggested that the training a dietitian receives is adequate preparation for entry level work and that private practice is considered beyond entry level. However, even in my Master's level education in nutrition, the topic of private practice was noticeably absent. My lack of resources and knowledge on the subject was the primary reason I didn't pursue this path when I was ready to move on from previous jobs.

When I searched for books on starting a nutrition practice, I was disappointed by how few resources there were for someone like me. I ended up receiving the "Entrepreneurial Nutritionist" by Kathy King as a gift and even though it was chock full of information, it wasn't exactly the resource I was hoping for. It was almost too broad.

Nutritionist In Private Practice

I didn't want to patent a nutrition device or consult for a sports team, long term care or health food stores. It was all very objective and useful knowledge, but it was missing a key element that I was desperate to understand. I really wanted to know the real life experience of someone who started their own nutrition business. I wanted to hear the story of how it happened. I wanted a glimpse inside the life of a nutritionist who was able to successfully transition to private practice.

So here, I offer you the resource I was searching for years ago, an honest account of my personal experience in getting started in business as a self employed nutritionist. The ideas, the motivation, the mistakes and surprises of the past couple of years are all here for you to read and enjoy. May it give you the courage to follow your dreams, knowing that it's possible to do work that you love and have it support you.

CHAPTER ONE

How I Knew Starting My Own Practice Was the Right Decision

"We're going to be moving to Colorado" I told my manager. It was that time of year again, when I got to speak my thoughts about my position and how I felt the job was going. We were in the middle of my annual performance evaluation. I was a valued team member and excelling in my job as a health coach. Needless to say, I was nervous about bringing up the subject. Putting the blame on an impending move seemed the logical way to go. It was true my husband and I had decided to move out of state, though it wasn't happening immediately. The truth was I was ready to leave my job. When it got to the part where I was asked, "So, is there anything you'd like to contribute?" That's when I dropped the bomb.

After four years of working for the company, there I was having the conversation about me having to leave. More accurately put, it was a conversation about me needing to leave. Needing to walk away from my dream job helping employees reach their wellness goals and improving their health status through nutrition. The funny thing is that I loved my coworkers and loved being a corporate dietitian health coach but there was something critically missing in my career. I couldn't put my finger on it exactly, but it was like I was constantly unsatisfied. I would get bored. I wanted to do more, create more, learn more. I just wanted more.

Have you ever worked a job for a few years, learned the ropes, then thought "what's next?" Or maybe it's more like "I love what I do, but I want to do it MY way." That was definitely me. You see, I had all these great ideas that I wanted to execute, but those decisions were never up to me, they had to be approved by 3 or 4 other levels of vested interests. Half the time, once an idea got support, there was barely enough time to execute it properly. I felt ready to break free from creative constraints. I wanted to explore ideas without asking for permission. I wanted to try new approaches, even if they weren't mainstream dogma.

How about this scenario: You've been at work and had some tasks to complete that took up about 3 hours of your working day, but then you had to stay busy for the remaining 5 hours while you were at the office. Have you ever wished you could just go home after your appointments were done? Why do we have to stay "on call" in the office?

And what about planning vacation time with your work team? How many sacrifices have you made in your vacation planning because you only had a certain allotment of permitted days off?

It was all of these little niggling things that just got to me over the years of working a typical nine to five day of the 40 hour workweek. Having to abide by the expected workday schedule, the holiday schedule, even the dress code got to me sometimes. And then there was the whole lack of advancement thing as a dietitian. Waiting all year to make just a little bit more in my paycheck. I counted myself lucky that I would get regular raises, but for an extra $40 or so per paycheck it didn't seem like much in the long run. I wanted more direct control over my future and I didn't feel like I had that as an employee.

The truth is, I had been thinking this way for awhile. Back in the Spring of 2013 I had taken a course in starting an online business. It was called B-School, and it had quite a following. It also was quite an investment. I can remember so clearly making the decision to go through with the program. I knew that having my own business was a long time dream, with the potential to become a reality with the right coaching, training and tools. B-School promised to teach me many of those things and I knew that making this decision was actually an investment in my dream. It felt as though signing up for B-School was the first step in my journey to entrepreneurship, and it was going to change the way I thought about myself.

Little by little, I started to implement the things I learned in the course. I created a website. I started a blog. I started getting my name out there, letting people know that I had a business. Of course, I was doing all of this on the side of my regular job. When I had downtime, I would write blog posts or work on the cookbook I was designing. It was the safe and smart way to go about it. I thought that I would be able to gradually build up some clientele and revenue on the side and eventually transition out of my full time job by the time my husband and I were ready to move to Colorado.

Something interesting started to happen during this period. Even though there was just a mere subtle shift in my daily work habits, a bigger shift occurred in my mindset. I began to think of myself as more of an entrepreneur. I thought "I bet some other professionals would like to collaborate with me!" "I have a unique skillset to offer." I felt more brave, daring, adventurous, enterprising. I began to think of ways I could get more exposure in the community and started introducing myself as a dietitian who sees clients (outside of my normal weekday job setting).

One of the strategic things I did during this time was attending a local Health and Wellness Expo. Normally I would have gone to this event for fun and learning, but this time I went for the networking. I was now Amy, the Entrepreneur. I even brought business cards. I spoke to a dozen other complementary health and wellness professionals and asked if their clients were interested in nutrition services. I offered how I could help with workshops and classes. Since I was still working full time, that's all I could offer, but I knew it would be a first step to getting my foot in the door. It was a great experience. Some practices were moderately interested, some seemed quite interested. I swapped quite a few cards, shared ideas and got energized to what I might pursue over the summer. Two businesses wanted to keep in touch about a potential partnership, so I held on tight to those names and followed up a few weeks later.

One of the opportunities didn't work out, but the other one seemed to be exactly what I was looking for. The business owner was setting up a new wellness center just outside of town. She was quite knowledgeable in herbs and alternative therapies and already had a successful supplement store in another town. She was creating her dream business with health spa treatments, supplements and services from other health professionals such as chiropractic treatment, massage, skin care and she was looking for a nutritionist and life coach to round out her business. Hello, that's me!! When we met to discuss the opportunity, I vividly remember walking into the building, the aromatherapy, the bubbling fountain, the peaceful flute music... I felt like my vision of working in a wellness center was coming true right before my eyes. The discussion was so energized, the business owner was so positive and encouraging. We worked out an arrangement where I would rent out office space and could conduct my services as I desired.

Everything about it seemed ideal and full of potential. As I walked out of the building after our initial meeting, I texted my husband immediately, "I'm about to make a life changing decision- will tell you more when I get home." Leasing out office space was a big financial commitment for me. I knew that I could technically afford it because I still had my full time job. My plan to drum up business was to teach classes in the evening and on weekends at the wellness center to build my client base. I thought by the end of the summer I would be ready to quit my other job. The timeline was suddenly moving along much quicker than expected, and I was just fine with that!

Just as I was getting giddy from my surge of enthusiasm and excitement, the first dark thoughts of doubt began to creep in. Was it really wise to leave the secure world of corporate America, the comfort and consistency of a salaried paycheck, the predictable schedule, the identity of corporate health coach nutritionist? Maybe I would miss the big beautiful buildings and fancy chairs, cozy office brunches and company provisions like my personal laptop, cell phone, expense accounts and paid trips to New York City and the mountains of the Virginia Blue Ridge Parkway. Was this really the world I was ready to leave behind? Did I dare speak the idea aloud? What if it was a huge mistake? What if I failed and had to explain my actions? There were so many what ifs whispering threats in my head, but there was also a louder voice fighting to make itself heard.

I imagined what it might look like to have my own business. The sense of freedom was the first thing that struck me. I would be my own boss! That definitely had a strong appeal. But I was also drawn to the vast potential for growth, development and creativity. I could make my business into anything I wanted. I could create anything I wanted and conduct my appointments in a flow that fit my style. I would be able to create a lifestyle that I valued. The flexibility I was seeking in my schedule and day to day flow would allow me to put attention into other areas of my life that were equally important to me. Working would no longer take up more than its share of hours in my week. My personal "wheel of life" would become more balanced and that felt right to me.

When I thought about doing my own thing and having my own business my energy went through the roof. My excitement was contagious. I wanted to tell everyone I knew about my plans and could barely sit still or sleep for days. I tried to think of any other job I would enjoy just to see if maybe there was something else out there that would grab my attention. But no, this was it. My own business was what I was really craving deep down. Making that dream a reality became my new obsession.

Lessons Learned:

- Listen to my inner voice that kept whispering, nagging me to do something else.

- Go where my energy grows. If working in a cubicle sucks the life out of me but I perk up when I think of writing a book, I need to follow that feeling.

CHAPTER TWO

Assessing the Market

> *"The last thing I heard is that Blue Cross is reimbursing dietitians $93 per unit of nutrition therapy provided, but I certainly suggest you confirm this."* My eyes bugged out of my head at the email I just read from my former dietitian colleague. I kept reading. *"Most BCBS covers 4 nutrition visits per year up to 6 with a diabetes diagnosis."* Hold the phone. I needed more information. I needed to talk to someone who was actually living this. I needed to find an actual nutritionist in private practice in North Carolina who I could talk to. It's one thing to have the logistics seem promising, but talking to someone who's making this work is the validation I needed to pursue this idea.

I was still bothered by the fear that it might not be possible to support myself while being self employed. For some reason, I worried there would be some kind of a legal hang up or too many hoops to jump through to make this dream happen. I worried that having my own practice wouldn't be reliable, predictable, or as financially stable as my regular job. I had to dispel these fears in order to take action forward. I needed to appease my rational brain with facts and figures. Initially, I decided to start on a part time basis. I would give myself plenty of time to build up clientele and then I could make the move to go part time at my salaried job instead of quitting entirely. It was the low risk way to proceed. I could work weekends (during the summers I had Fridays off) and by the end of the summer I could re-evaluate where I was at with my transition.

Talking to others already successful and knowledge-able on the subject was on my list to help make this idea a viable reality. After doing a little online research, I found a few local dietitians that I contacted via email and even managed to set up a couple of phone conversations. Their time and feedback was worth their weight in gold. I just needed to know for sure that it was possible, that real people were doing it and making a living. It only took a couple of conversations before I was off, raring to go. Everything they said made it sound like it was fairly simple, straight-forward and doable. I decided to go ahead and take action to pursue contracts with a few insurance companies and open my very own nutrition practice in Greensboro, North Carolina.

Even though my decision was made and things were set in motion, I reminded myself to be conservative about my transition. At the time, my current work schedule during the summer was 4 ten hour days. I had Fridays off, and I thought I could ease into it by seeing clients on Fridays and the weekend. It would give me a couple of months to get things going, get my contracts set and then I could reassess in September to see if I would be ready to go down to part time status at my job. It definitely felt more responsible and much less panicky to take this approach and let the business and clients build up first.

Lessons Learned:

- Make sure there are others to talk to who have successfully done it.

- Decrease stress of starting my business by making a gradual transition.

CHAPTER THREE

Brick and Mortar or Virtual Practice?

"If I have my own office, I could see people right here in town. I already know a lot of people and have been in this community for the past five years. It makes sense to have a local practice." The voices were speaking in my head again. As much as I hoped to achieve the dream of having a completely mobile, location independent online business, the reality is that I had no history online. I had dabbled in some blogging and had created an Etsy shop to sell my extra wares after a craft show, but other than that, I didn't really have a following. I had still yet to create my message and attract the people who wanted to hear it. That took time. I really wanted out of the corporate world now. I really wanted to have my own business, and the fastest track was to get started with who I already knew, my local community. I could develop my online business along the way.

A significant influence in my decision to start my own business was an online marketing course I took earlier that spring called B-School. It had always been in the back of my mind to eventually find a way to shift into online work for the flexibility and accessibility. I dreamed of being able to work from my laptop from my back deck or even from a beachfront. As a student of this course I learned quite a bit about social media marketing, email lists and website functionality, but the most valuable lesson I learned was to take action steps towards your dreams. Act like the person you want to become, even if you are not there yet. The course gave me a big jump start in developing the online presence of my business. My website, my concept and my products and programs were thought out and created before my local practice had even opened its doors.

Instead of choosing between the two options of building an online business or opening a local practice, I decided to pursue both. Even though B-School gave me all the necessary tools to "know what to do and how to do it" in order to become successful online, it also was an option that would take much more time to solidly develop, and I didn't have that. The creator of B-School, Marie Forleo, mentions that it took her about 10 years to become highly profitable in the online world. In my mind, I had already given my notice at my career job and wanted a faster transition. I knew that I could still build up an online presence, offer products, programs and services online and it would be a great support to my private practice.

One advantage I had in opening a physical office for my practice was that I live in a relatively large area with a population close to 250,000. I knew that I had the population density to have clients of many types, including those within my specialties. The other advantage I had was that I had many contacts within the health industry which had potential as a source for referrals. Having a local business also came with one more important advantage. Seeing clients face to face permitted the option of contracting with insurance companies for providing medical nutrition therapy which was something I was considering doing.

Lesson Learned:

- I can't rush developing a new business. It takes even more time to develop an online business. Putting most of my energy into a local practice while slowly building the online one would get me going faster, especially since my local community was large.

CHAPTER FOUR

Deciding Whether or Not to Take Insurance

"Is it really true? Do people with Blue Cross insurance plans actually get unlimited visits?" I asked, astounded at the idea. "Yes, it's really true!" she said. I was on the phone with another dietitian who had her own local nutrition practice. I found her online and reached out to see if we could connect in person since I had so many questions about the process of taking insurance in my practice. The validation she provided ignited my inner-entrepreneur. Suddenly, it all seemed more sustainable and achievable. If I could find a good handful of clients who had this type of insurance and create a long term relationship, I wouldn't have to work so hard constantly finding new clients. "The new health care reform law changed the nutrition benefits for many plans," she explained, "Now, patients aren't limited by diagnosis, and they can come back as often as needed, provided that the care is medically necessary." In my head, I extrapolated the business model. More long

term (return) clients equals less marketing, less stress, improved relationships and increased client satisfaction. A win-win. Yes, I thought, this is worth figuring out. I'm totally doing this.

The idea for taking insurance had been floating around all summer as I discussed my intentions to start my own practice with other North Carolina RDs. One of the benefits of being a registered dietitian was that you can contract with insurance companies, submit claims for medical nutrition therapy and get reimbursed for this. It was certainly intriguing, but so many details were unknown, namely where to get started. In my earlier conversation with my former colleague I learned that Blue Cross Blue Shield was a great company to contract with in the state of North Carolina. She didn't know the exact details but told me they reimbursed dietitians "very well." She suggested contacting other practicing RDs to see if I could get more information.

Both of us weren't strangers to the process of contracting with insurance companies. When we worked together at UNC Hospital we had to apply for in-network credentialing with various insurers because of the billing group we were associated with in the outpatient diabetes education program. Aside from filling out a gazillion applications and forms, the billing associates in the clinic took care of the details. Through the process I had acquired a National Provider Identification number (NPI) and contracts with Medicare, Blue Cross Blue Shield, United Healthcare, Aetna and likely a few others that I can't remember. After that, whenever I saw a patient, I would place the appropriate code on their checkout papers and the clinic took care of the billing and payments. From that experience, it didn't seem so far fetched to simply update my contracts. I just needed to verify that it was possible.

I received a few good tips and resources from the North Carolina dietitians in private practice I contacted. One had an entire booklet outlining the credentialing and billing process on her website. It was pure gold! She was one of the contributing authors which is likely why she had it available for download on her site. It answered many of my questions about the process of how to get contracted and how to bill for services, but I still had a few concerns. I still didn't know how much I would get paid for a typical visit. I didn't know what kinds of restrictions there might be. I wasn't sure how complicated the billing process was, how long it took or how long it was before you got paid.

I ended up deciding that I would at least try. There would be nothing to lose by starting the process and if things didn't work out, I could still take cash. I figured that I would get the credentialing process started that summer so that I would hopefully have the process completed before Fall. According to my projected timeline, I'd have the option to go part time or even leave my job by then if things were going well.

In the process of getting credentialed I noticed there were a few changes since I went through the credentialing process at the hospital. There was a whole new online database called CAQH that apparently helped simplify the process by allowing you to submit all of your records to one clearinghouse. It added a layer of confusion to the process because I didn't understand I still had to send in applications to each insurance company separately. CAQH existed so that the insurance companies could verify who I was in one location. Then there was the confusion of my NPI number not matching my current married name. In all of my dealings, my NPI number identified where I was in the application process, but it was attached to my maiden name (from the hospital job) and not my married name. There was also a technical difficulty in my Tax-ID number on one of my applications. Each insurance company is different, but many state that it can take up to 30 business days to process an application. It was hard to gauge the progress on my applications, but when 30 days passed, I contacted the companies I hadn't heard from to find out the status. That's when I learned about the mix up of the last name and the Tax-ID number mismatch. It felt really frustrating and confusing and helpless to not understand why the process was taking so long. However, I've heard from others that they were able to get contracted in the 30 day period. I suppose I was just "lucky" with my technicalities. October rolled around and I was becoming so frustrated and dejected about the idea of getting contracted I had stopped thinking about it. I even had a client who was waiting to start working with me because she had Blue Cross Blue Shield insurance. She wanted to wait to meet until her insurance would cover it. I had to put her off for a month.

The funny thing is I finally got my letter from Blue Cross Blue Shield when I was on vacation in Hawaii. It was an urgent letter that needed signing and return and all I had was my smartphone! Luckily, I was able to electronically sign it and return, but I could barely read the contract on my phone. It also didn't help that it read in legalese. I still had no idea what I would be paid! The silver lining was that I could finally schedule an appointment with my client.

The other piece I learned when I was researching insurance companies is that not all companies contract with dietitians. When I called Cigna and United Healthcare, both said they did not contract with dietitians "in my area." I was shocked and disappointed. I was hoping I could offer to continue relationships with the clients I had in my health coaching job but didn't think it would be appealing to clients to have to start paying for service since their insurance wouldn't cover it.

After I got my Blue Cross Blue Shield contract, I received a few phone calls from potential clients looking for a dietitian in their area. Apparently, I was listed on the insurance website and they found my name in a directory. This was another advantage to being an in-network provider, greater visibility and marketing from the insurance company side.

I didn't think I would pursue any other contracts at first. I wanted to "practice" working with one and Blue Cross Blue Shield seemed to be one of the area's largest insurers. Someone had suggested that Blue Cross had the largest share of the market, and it seemed to be true. I didn't have trouble finding people (or people finding me) who had Blue Cross insurance. It was my husband who asked me if I would see people with Medicare insurance. He was a physician assistant in a local cardiology practice and came across quite a few candidates for nutrition consults. I did have a Medicare contract previously from the hospital, but knew I'd have to update my application to my own practice. I wasn't that motivated to start the process considering I was unsure how much trouble it would be and how long it would take. Also, Medicare has quite a few restrictions in what is covered for Medical Nutrition Therapy, namely that it covered MNT for diabetes and renal disease only. But the entrepreneur in me thought, "What do you have to lose? It's just paperwork." Plus, the fact that I was a Certified Diabetes Educator increased the likelihood that I could incur quite a few referrals made the idea worth exploring. Amazingly, it took less time to process the Medicare application than it did the Blue Cross one. I'm sure the process was greatly expedited because I already had a Medicare provider number from my previous job at the hospital.

The exciting thing I learned about working with insurance is that there has been a lot of advances in plan benefits over the past few years. Although it feels like ages ago, when I was a new dietitian in North Carolina, I remember being part of a group that tried to expand nutrition benefits as part of the Blue Cross Blue Shield plan. I was a warm body in the room (too new as an RD to really contribute much in the area of private practice) as discussions went around trying to engage dietitians in becoming contracted providers. At the time, I wasn't able to go into business for myself, but I remembered thinking "nutrition services are becoming more important, even the insurance companies are sitting down and changing their policies."

I noticed that at least one client had nutrition plan benefits that were not restricted by any particular diagnosis. There were no restrictions placed on number of visits. There was no copay or deductible! I almost couldn't believe that this was true. I reached out to one of the other NC private practice RDs I had spoken to before. "Is this really true? Can patients come as often as they want and not have to pay anything?" And she said, "Yep, it's really true!" It was at this moment that I saw the potential for true income from the insurance based practice model materialize in my mind. I could develop real, lasting relationships with my clients over the year and continue to help them with their progress. I had just assumed that most companies would have benefits similar to Medicare with a limit of 3 or 6 visits and limited to certain medical conditions. For the most part, I found that most in state Blue Cross Blue Shield plans had excellent benefits for nutrition therapy. Out of state plans usually had some visit limitations or required diagnosis, but often when I verified the plan benefits, I found that most people qualified for at least 6 visits.

As the year progressed I decided to look into a few more insurance companies and contracted with Aetna,

American Specialty Health and Optum Healthcare. The latter two were the wellness divisions of United Health-care and Cigna, both of which offered a cash discount to their members, but no specific coverage for nutrition. I also learned that sometimes insurance plans provided out of network benefits, so I could still see someone even if I was not "in-network"as a provider. For example, with United Medicare plans, most patients are allowed out of network MNT benefits if they have diabetes. For the most part, if you are out of network, there is usually a higher deductible, but if the patient has already met their out of network deductible for the year, then the MNT visit would be covered. It's always worth looking into the details of the individual's plan because you may find out it's a covered benefit, even if you're out of network.

The other thing I really enjoyed about working with insurance companies is that it created a much different dynamic in the client-provider relationship. I didn't have to do any convincing or sell my value to the client. The concept of covered visits, deductibles and out of network were terms people were familiar with, and they were usually willing to pay their part if needed. But for those who had 100% coverage, the topic of money was magically off the table. It was never something we had to address and we could just focus on their visit. Many of my clients would probably not seek out nutritional counseling if it was an additional expense. I was more than happy to be able to offer my services and work with their insurance company to provide the benefit. In retrospect, I credit my ability to take insurance as the single greatest contributor to my business success in my first year.

Lessons Learned:

- Verify that the major insurance companies in my area contract with dietitians. Once in network, the reimbursement is better and my listing appears in their directories.

- Start the paperwork process as soon as possible. It can take 1-3 months (possibly more) for contracts to be finalized.

- It's MUCH easier to get new and repeat clients when clients know there is insurance coverage for their visits.

CHAPTER FIVE

Collaborations, Networking and Highlighting my Speciality

"It would be a great service to our patients to have you here," the doctor said. "We're not looking to make any money off of you. With our patient volume and nutritional risk, I think you'll be as busy as you want to be. And you get the perk of working in the same building as your husband!" I was grinning. The head physician of the cardiology practice where my husband worked had requested a meeting to discuss the idea of having me work at their practice as an independent contractor. It was a quick meeting, but he officially gave the idea his blessing and assigned the practice manager to follow up on the details of me renting office space from them. It seemed like the perfect relationship. All of their patients were in need of nutrition counseling and a high percentage of them fulfilled the insur-

*ance requirements I needed for Medicare.
It would provide me with an endless source
of referrals. And working onsite meant that
I could see patients on demand, if I had any
schedule openings.*

One of my biggest worries about going out on my own was that I thought it meant spending long hours and many dollars marketing myself. Was I going to have to spend hundreds of dollars on print ads or radio spots? Was I going to be hanging flyers all around the town? There was a bit of desperation to be seen and known. Some of that desperation and worry led me to make some hasty decisions.

When I decided to rent out office space at the wellness center, there was also an implicit agreement to partner together to promote the center and the services within. I held a few workshops before the grand opening weekend in September to draw in clients and promote my services. The turnout was small, but a couple of attendees seemed interested in pursuing individual nutrition consults. I also offered to sign them up for my newsletter. Otherwise, business was slow at the wellness center. The chiropractor had a few steady clients and others would come in for detox services, but overall business seemed sluggish. I reminded myself that it was a new business getting estab- lished, so I kept my optimism high.

The grand opening brought in many vendors and lots of faces that seemed excited about the new wellness center. Tours were given and raffles were drawn and several appointments were booked for services. However, the majority of services that were promoted during the open house were the detox treatments and chiropractic appointments. I didn't make as many connections on grand opening day. My booth wasn't in the main traffic area and people weren't super eager to book nutrition sessions. At the time, I hadn't finalized my insurance contracts, so I wasn't able to advertise that option yet. A couple of people did sign up for the nutrition workshop, but I had much higher expectations for the big marketing event. The owner, chiropractor and massage therapist were thrilled with the business they'd generated for themselves, but I had a hard time sharing in their excitement. For some reason, I didn't have the same experience.

Passing time revealed more details about the status of the wellness center. The grand opening was in September and over the course of October and November, not much new business was coming in. In December, the chiropractor (who was pretty much the anchor service provider) left and moved her business out of state. There wasn't much else driving new clients to the center at that point. The owner remained hopeful that new business would come in by the new year and we would spend afternoons brainstorming fun ways to engage clients, like weekend retreats and spa days.

In the meantime, I had engaged in talks with the head partner of the cardiology practice my husband worked in. The cardiologist was interested in having me come into their practice to offer my services to their patients. I had to really think about this offer. Although it was my husband's suggestion that I talk with them, I wasn't sure that it would be a source of ideal clients. However, it had the potential to be a huge source of revenue. Close to a hundred patients a day are seen in the practice. The arrangement would allow for me to rent space and see referred patients either the same day or scheduled in advance. There were several factors to analyze regarding this opportunity.

In the "pros" column, there were many advantages. I would have a consistent source of endless referrals. I would have referrals for clients who have insurance. I would have a higher likelihood of getting patients with diabetes which would allow me to bill Medicare. I would be affiliated with a highly respected, well known, well established cardiology practice. I would be working in the same practice as my husband. I was familiar with and liked the other providers in the group. The "cons" list wasn't quite as long, but it did give me hesitation. One, I was already in a signed lease with the wellness center. I wanted to avoid paying two rents. I was also afraid of becoming too busy. I had a fear of being booked solid, day in and day out, which would eliminate the flexibility I was hoping for by opening my own practice. I also wasn't sure the environment was an ideal match. It was a full fledged cardiology practice with really sick patients. I hadn't worked in a clinic environment since I was at the hospital, which I left so I could focus on the prevention and wellness side of nutrition.

However, the opportunity was available. That was

enough to think about for now without having to make a hasty decision. The practice manager was coordinating the logistics. I thought I could make it work if I was part time in both office locations. The cardiology practice would provide the income to help make up for the wellness center, but the wellness center would provide the environment I was seeking while giving me a little schedule flexibility.

In the meantime I saw a referral from my husband at the wellness center and picked up a couple of more clients who were referrals from the Blue Cross Blue Shield website. By the end of December I had seen about 5 clients. It was enough to give me the confidence that my business was actually growing. I made the decision to tell my manager at my salaried job that I was ready to have January be my last month of employment. I had started a mediation program that Fall that I wanted to see through one more month, so I kept working 1 day a week in January so I could continue to host the meditation group and help create a smooth transition as I left the position.

Around the same time, I found out that there was another practice interested in partnering with me. In the same building as the wellness center was a privately owned pharmacy. The wellness center chiropractor told me they were excited to hear that a registered dietitian had opened an office in the building. They were also an accredited diabetes education center and saw quite few patients with diabetes. We scheduled a time to meet and chat in January and it came up that they were interested in having me assist teaching the diabetes classes. I was quite interested in the idea, it gave me a little more stability at the wellness center office location and would also give me exposure to more potential clients. I also liked the idea that they were already established and had an ongoing program that was accredited.

January was a pivotal month in my business. I discussed changing my lease terms with the owner of the wellness center to allow me to pay for part time use of the space on a month to month basis. She understood that I was trying to make the arrangement at the cardiology practice work and depending on the lease agreement that was decided there, I would decide whether to keep the office space with her. I decided to pursue the partnership with the pharmacy. I would be independent and not be paid to teach the classes. However, I would be able to bill insurance for group nutrition visits and then follow up with individuals as needed. The cardiology practice was the hold up. They had recently merged with the area hospital system and it made the proposed arrangement much more complicated. My emails from the practice manager were getting ignored, and I was not getting answers about the status of the arrangement. I continued to see referrals from the practice at my other office location, but it was 20 miles outside of town, so not exactly convenient for patients in town.

It was February when I found out that the wellness center was closing. The owner decided to cut her losses and move her inventory and equipment back to her other location as she was unable to find new practitioners or drum up additional business for herself. She had made me an offer to buy out her inventory at a huge discount but the thought of taking on additional responsibilities including more rent, inventory and marketing a business that had no solid, existing clientele was absolutely unappealing to me. She was concerned for my welfare and had spoken to the pharmacy owner, who owned the entire building. After the wellness center closed, the arrangement would be that I could move my office into the pharmacy conference room. We negotiated the terms to be a mutual swap for services. I would teach the diabetes class and help lead the diabetes support group and he would provide me office space to use two days per week. At this point, two days a week was all I needed to see all the existing clients I had. And I loved the idea of not having to pay rent. I began to feel more invested with being a team member in the pharmacy diabetes program and knew that even though the wellness center didn't work out the way I had hoped, it was a stepping stone to a better arrangement.

By March I learned that my partnership with the cardiology practice wasn't going to happen. Too much was going on with the hospital merger to push myself into the scene as an unofficial staff member. The hospital was a juggernaut that I didn't want to deal with, so I made peace with the fact that it didn't work out. The silver lining was that between my husband and the head practice physician, I had quite an endorsement in the practice as the preferred dietitian for patient referrals. I had created my own referral sheets and gave them to my husband along with my business cards so that he would place them in the clinic rooms so providers would have easy access to my information. The referral sheet was simple; patient name, contact info and physician signature was all that I asked for. My husband would collect these and bring them home for me to call the patient and follow up on the referral. It was a fairly simple system, but it has worked well. I've had probably close to 50 percent of my clients come from referrals from the cardiology practice and that's without being onsite in their office.

Because my actual office was 20 miles out of town, I began to feel the need to have a second office space in town. I had received a couple of declinations from potential clients because they didn't want to travel out of town to see me. I began to look around and see what options there were. I spoke with my massage therapist who used to rent space at my chiropractor's office and she suggested I speak with her to see what options she had. This idea was appealing to me because the office was very close to my house and I was familiar with the office staff as well. We had a quick conversation where she suggested I speak to the owner but otherwise was excited to have me in the office with my practice. The process took just a couple of week to arrange, but I was able to sign a very reasonable lease and start seeing patients in my new location in April. The timing was perfect because I had just committed to marketing my business at the Health and Wellness Expo this year and wanted to appeal to local residents.

Trying to figure out who best to align myself with to

promote my business has been quite a learning curve. The funny thing is that where I tried the hardest to make it work is where it least succeeded. My biggest successful partnerships came from the suggestions of others. Even though it didn't workout to be in the cardiology practice, I now have a nice referral stream from them. And even though the wellness center didn't work out, it allowed me to partner with the pharmacy and keep an office location in an area out of town that broadened my service area. I estimate that in the past year about 80% of my clients have come from referrals from other practices including the diabetes program I teach. About 20% come from self referrals who find my information on insurance website directories, my own website or from me promoting my services. Clients seem to trust word of mouth recommendations over self promotion. I'm sure that if I were solely responsible for marketing my services, I would have been working much harder and possibly not been quite as successful.

Lessons Learned:

- It saves lots of time marketing to be affiliated with another practice, or complementary business that has a similar client base. I did not have to market myself much at all.

- Don't partner with a new business owner who is depending on me to drive new clients their business.

CHAPTER SIX

How to Set Up Shop: Technology and Tools Used

"Surely I'm forgetting something," I thought. It just didn't seem right to walk out of the house with just my ipad. Just a few months ago it was typical for me to carry multiple bags and belongings with me. Sometimes it took multiple trips to pack up the car, just to go to work. It all depended on how strong I felt and how much I felt like I could carry. My purse, my lunchbag, my laptop and charger, my rolling travel bag that contained files, a scale, automatic blood pressure cuff and glucometer, my gym bag with change of clothes, hair dryer, shoes and toiletries and a towel. That was a typical day of getting ready to go to work. For three years I had a job with a commute that also involved periodic out of town travel. I remember the yearning was so strong for a simpler way. "Why do I need so many bags? Why is there so much stuff??" When the moment

came that I realized how streamlined my new business had become, it seemed so foreign, such an alien feeling to walk out of the house with one single item. It felt like a dream. The feeling of levity, the freedom it symbolized was at the core of what I was searching for in simplifying my work.

One thing that is appealing in being a dietitian is that you don't need a whole lot of equipment to do your thing. I can literally conduct a quality consult with just a good listening ear and a way to take notes. In the past few years, the electronic medical record has made keeping paper charts irrelevant. To get started though, I had cost concerns that I wanted to be cautious about. Keeping paper records seemed easy enough and the lowest cost way to start out. I had a bunch of file folders and made copies of intake forms that I would use in the first visit. Then I had a different form I would use to chart on for follow up visits. I had clients sign a HIPPA form and a medical records release form. The paperwork was really quite minimal. Legally, I just needed to keep the health information protected and private, which meant locking notes in a cabinet or office. This was easy for me to do in a private office.

As I got busier, it ended up being the scheduling and record keeping that became more complicated. The notes and charting were fairly straightforward. Even though I find it easier to review chart notes as a paper file, I needed a system where I could schedule patients, look up their contact details and ideally give them appointment reminders. While at the wellness center, we were all using MindBody, an app that coordinated clients and scheduled appointments. I used it for scheduling, reminders and to look up phone numbers from time to time. But after the wellness center went away, I was in the market for a new system. I hunted online and think I googled something like "client scheduling app" and landed upon DrChrono.

It seemed to have everything I was looking for and it was free! More specifically, there was a free version of the software that was so robust, it met 99% of my needs. Not only did it provide a client database and scheduling system it also was able to send email reminders and interfaced with iphone and ipad. Then I realized the best feature of all of the system….the ability to customize and chart using an electronic medical record. I could now switch to e-charting! At first I was concerned I would faced with double work. I'd have to take my handwritten notes from the visit and then put them into the record after the face and it would create added administration time. But cleverly, with DrChrono the charting could be done via ipad- which meant I could take notes discretely during the visit! Having an ipad handy made the whole process quite mobile and I could maintain good eye contact and not have a computer screen in the way.

I did receive a tip from another dietitian in private prac-tice about which billing system to use. She suggested Office Ally. It was free to use and they also offered other features such as practice management and claims reconciliation. All I needed was a place to be able to enter and submit my claims through Medicare, as I had not yet established my Medicare provider portal account. Office Ally is essentially a clearing house where one can enter an insurance claim with the corresponding insurance company and insured's information and they will submit the claim for you and alert you to the status. They will even submit a paper claim if necessary and charge a very small fee for this service. What I like about Office Ally is that they store your personal and patient information, so you don't need to re-enter it every time. It also allowed me the option to submit claims from other insurance companies that I did not have contracts with. For example, I am out of network with United Healthcare, but an in-network Medicare provider. I've had many patients who have a Medicare plan that has been replaced by United, creating a sort of combo plan. I wasn't entirely sure if I would be reimbursed through these plans, but I was able to find out by trial and error. Office Ally is a must for submitting claims electronically when you don't have direct access to a provider portal account direct from the insurance company. Later, I was able to get a provider portal access with United Healthcare, even as an out of network provider, so I use Office Ally for just a few insurance companies that have Medicare combo plans and one other company I am contracted with but have no provider portal access. The only other essential tool I realized I needed was a small notebook where I kept track of my claim submissions and reimbursements.

I had other various tools that I use like a tape measure, a body fat analyzer some favorite handouts and resources for diabetes, cholesterol and meal plan guides, but I tended to customize for each individual and provide lot of website and book references in my visits. I had no need to carry around a lot of equipment with me every time I go to the office. This was nice considering I had 2 offices and wouldn't want to bring a bookcase of materials with me everywhere. One nice feature of having one office in the pharmacy where we teach diabetes classes is that there are lots of props there like food models and food labels handy if needed. My other office at the chiropractic center had a few decorations on the walls, framed license and credentials, 2 lightweight armchairs and a storage ottoman where I keep all my handouts. The chairs were about $100 each and was the biggest overhead investment for me getting started.

Day to day I would carry my ipad and sometimes my laptop with me to work. If I'm planning to be there much of the day it's nice to have the laptop to work off of, but otherwise I only bring my ipad with me if I just have a few appointments. Since I got the Omron body fat analyzer, it's one more thing to carry, so I have a separate pouch where I keep that, a tape measure, BMI index wheel and some business cards. I really don't carry much else. The bulk of my handouts are at the office and can utilize a notepad and paper if need. I didn't need to invest in any more capital or tools for the rest of the year.

Lessons Learned:

- Make sure to budget for essentials, but there are many unexpected low cost or free tools worth using.

- Don't overspend on supplies and office furniture. I needed less than I thought.

- Add as my practice grew. I was able to add additional services and tools gradually.

CHAPTER SEVEN

Getting Additional Business Support

"We should totally start a mastermind group!" My friend who I had met from the book club was radiant with enthusiasm. "We are already so close and on similar journeys in starting our own businesses. It would be a great way to keep in touch after the book club is over and we could have the collective wisdom of amazing, brilliant women," she explained. The serendipity was almost too much to bear. I loved the idea, and I had been thinking the same thing about the women I had come to know over the past month. "You know, I'm right there with you. This has to happen," I said. "I had been wanting to find a mastermind group to be part of. And the fact that it's all women, we should call it a Wisdom Circle!" I knew how much value there was in having accountability for growing a business. I'd been working with a personal business coach for the past few months which was amazing, but the prospect of having a circle of trusted friends there to support me and

my business ideas had me thrilled. "I envision five wise women as part of this group," my friend described. "Who do you think could be a part of this group?" I smiled. "I have some ideas," I nodded, my smile growing wider. "And I think they'll be just as excited as we are about this collective."

It can be a lonely road as an entrepreneur. Especially if you find yourself working from home several days a week. You may not have the social contact you've been accustomed to in a traditional job. Without the constructs of a workplace team environment or manager directing your deadlines, it can also be hard to follow through on deadlines you set for yourself. This is where seeking additional support can be quite valuable, especially if you're just starting out in your business. Support can come in many forms, starting simply with an "accountability partner." This would be someone like a peer who is on a similar track. You would meet as often as you'd like, to help keep each other supported. The benefit of this arrangement is that it doesn't cost anything and you get the accountability and ideas from each other.

You can also apply this to a group format, often referred to as a "mastermind" where the collective input is shared from many individuals. Often these are free, but some may charge money, as another way to elevate the value of the group. Sometimes they are led by a mentor, and you may be paying for the expertise of the mastermind leader. These may not meet as frequently due to logistics. There's also the option of hiring a coach or mentor, someone who has more expertise than you on a subject. Getting one to one personalized attention usually comes at a premium, but it can also be the most effective in generating action and big change in developing your business. Meetings are typically weekly, but can vary based on the agreement.

Even though I just got done saying that you can keep your investments to a minimum when you first get started, I consider hiring a business coach as a "nice to have" investment, not an essential tool. I felt like I needed an experienced advisor for weekly support, accountability, ideas, and to basically have someone who's been in my shoes be able to guide me along my journey in developing my online business. The local practice was humming right along, so I felt the need to put more attention into my online strategy and overall business brand. I met my business coach in the B-School online community, which was full of experienced entrepreneurs. I purchased a three month coaching program from her, and we met weekly over Skype to discuss my business vision, strategy and offerings.

Over the course of our relationship, she helped me to outline what I wanted my year to look like. What would my key offerings be? What would my signature program consist of? All of this was based on the goal income I wanted to make from my business. So I picked a number that seemed reasonable, $50,000. This was my goal for all online business income. From this figure, we had to look at what would generate the income to reach that goal. I decided on creating a couple of coaching packages, one for nutrition and one for mentoring other nutritionists. Then, I wanted to work on creating a signature program. This took up the bulk of my free time when I was not actually seeing clients in my local practice. So was it worth it to hire a business coach? Absolutely, yes. It gave me undivided weekly attention from a mentor who held space for me to brainstorm and develop my business ideas outside of a local practice. Weekly "homework" kept me accountable to keep making progress in something that can easily get overwhelming. If it wasn't for my coach, I wouldn't have developed my programs on time, I wouldn't have held any webinars or had the clarity to describe what exactly it is that I offer my clients. The relationship helped me to stay engaged in visualizing exactly what it was that I wanted to develop and not run out of steam before I completed it. She ended up being a tremendous resource for me and continues to be a trusted colleague in the online business world.

The other business support system that developed that year was a local business support group. Many people refer to these as "Mastermind" groups, where you benefit from the collective wisdom of all participants. However, we decided to call our group a Women's Wisdom Circle, since we were all female and had an appreciation for our innate wisdom to guide us. We originally met through a book club I hosted, and as that meeting came to an end, we noticed that many of us in the group were in a similar situation. We were all trying to develop our own businesses. It only took a suggestion of the idea to generate the enthusiasm to create the group. We decided to meet every week for 3 months, with a few of these meetings being over an online meeting platform.

I went from having a weekly business coach for 3 months to weekly group business support meetings for another 3 months! The support, the fellowship and authentic caring for the success of each other's endeavors was amazing. It was just as exciting to see a friend's business idea take off as it was to share my own wins for the week. Even after the three months ended, we couldn't bear to end our engagement, so we decided to keep meeting monthly as able. Not every member made it to every meeting, but the support system was still there in spirit.

The Wisdom Circle Mastermind group made developing my business feel like less of a tactical plan and more of an intuitive discovery. I learned that I actually was less interested in aggressively developing and marketing an online nutrition business and had other interests in arts and crafts that I was more interested in exploring. The advice we gave each other wasn't based in MBAs, proven systems or strategic alliances. We used our intuition, felt guided by heart and let our emotions have a say in the directions we suggested for each other. For so many of us, this approach proved fruitful despite how uncomfortable or unprofessional it can be to take action on an instinct or feeling.

Through the experience of my new year in business, I felt well guided and supported, which is something I would wish for any entrepreneur starting out. It can be a difficult and emotionally challenging road to attempt on your own, and having extra support for those times helped me to not give up and to keep trying, even when I felt like I didn't know what I was doing. Every single time I left from a group meeting or one to one coaching session I felt like I had recharged my batteries from the universe. I was renewed with confidence, hope, innovation and courage to put myself out there and make my business a success. This feeling alone made the monetary and time investment in these support systems worth it.

Lessons Learned:

- It's worth investing in a support system. It was worth money for someone to mentor me and worth the time invested in group support to stay on track with goals.

- It's natural to have energetic and emotional ups and downs as an entrepreneur. Having a support network has been priceless in helping me navigate the waves.

CHAPTER EIGHT

A Typical Day in the Life of an Entrepreneur

It's so quiet. A few cars go by, on their way to work. I hear the birds. The bus comes by and loads up the school kids. One of the first things I notice in the morning is the quiet pace I've grown accustomed to. No loud alarm clock to start the day. No music to get me going out the door. No rushing, packing bags, or prepping a lunchbox. It's all become a more leisurely pace. I put on cozy pants and a sweater (my loungewear for the day) and fix a cup of tea. I contemplate breakfast and typically decide on bacon and eggs. I catch up online and plan out of my schedule for the day. Starting with the big ticket items first, and the rest will fill itself in between appointments. Ooh, I just had someone reschedule. No worries, I'll be able to get more writing done instead.

A question I get frequently is "what do you do in a typical day?" Although it's a pretty natural question, it's not one with an easy or consistent answer. It depends on several variables, one being the day of the week. The beauty of having your own business is that you have a flexible schedule, but it can easily be completely different day to day and week to week; you really need to be prepared for that. Some weeks my office at the pharmacy is the busier location, especially if the diabetes class is going on. I've had some 10 hour days, but that's really not typical. Most of my days start off like the paragraph above.

On some days I only have a couple of appointments scheduled, so I spend the rest of the day catching up on administrative details, finishing charting notes, calling and scheduling referral patients, calling the insurance company to verify benefits or find out about a claim that was denied. I always have other things to work on, especially in regards to the online piece of the business whether it be an article to write, or a book to finish! Recently, there's been several edits and adjustments to the curriculum of the diabetes class, so I work on that from time to time.

When I'm not working on the business, I often have hobby business stuff to attend to: orders from my Etsy shop to fulfill, products to make, classes to take. I'm also quite busy raising a German Shepherd puppy, keeping him active and entertained. Through the summer when business was slower I would take him to the dog park for a couple of hours at a time. I would feel conflicted that I should be home working on a blog post article or developing my next online program, but my gut kept bringing me back to enjoying the day and enjoying my dog when he was at this particular stage in life. He was so full of curiosity, energy and needing attention. The business growth took a back seat and I was able to trust in the process enough to let it run on autopilot. One of the true joys of having your own schedule is being able to prioritize the important things in life more easily.

I did find it much more challenging after getting a puppy to maintain any type of regular schedule or routine when working from home. I used to be able to sit on the couch and bang out good quality writing or brainstorm a program with some peace and quiet, but I really don't have that luxury anymore. It's probably a similar situation most parents raising young children have as they find their attention split between home duties and working on the business. I realized that I if I really needed to get quality work done, I actually have to curb my time working from home and utilize my offices more to have a distraction free environment.

Example of a Typical Day:

Wake up around 7 to say goodbye to my husband as he goes to work or sleep in until 8 if I'm really tired.

Have tea & decide my plan of action for the day.

Go to the gym for a morning workout.

Come home by 10am and have a late breakfast.

Take the dog for a walk.

Get some work done on the computer: checking emails, social media, look at my to-do list for today and examine my priorities.

Clean up the house & play with the dog or take him to the park if no early appointments.

Get ready for a day at the office (pack a lunch for a longer day). Longer days at the office may omit some morning activities I don't have time for.

See 2-4 clients on average.

Keep up with charting notes, billed claims and referrals in between clients.

Come home, tend to the dog and prepare dinner.

Do some evening activity: Follow up on social media, work on a crafty project, prep for the next day.

Some days of the week there are set schedules. For awhile it was bi-weekly business mastermind meetings on Friday mornings. Then I was taking art classes at night on Tuesdays for six weeks. I lead a diabetes support group bi-monthly on the first Tuesday of the month. I occasionally see a client or two on a Saturday. Once a month the two week diabetes class is held on Wednesday evenings. Most Mondays and Tuesdays I see evening clients. What I like best is that it's all up to me. If I don't want to see clients at 8am, I encourage them to schedule later. If I feel like earning income on the weekend, I'll see clients on a Saturday. If I want to take a special class, I can rearrange my schedule without much trouble to make room for interests that are important to me.

Lessons Learned:

- No day is typical, but don't let that be an excuse to be unstructured about being self employed. I still needed structure and routines to stay productive and healthy.

- My schedule is in my hands. I can prioritize what's most important to me and still have time to see enough clients to make the income I need.

CHAPTER NINE

Money Fears Unfounded, Analyzing Patterns

*"Don't worry about money. I've been sav-
ing a little extra and have some tucked
away in my savings account," my husband
said softly. This may have been one of the
sweetest gestures my husband made in regards to me starting my own practice. "And
if it doesn't work out, I can always get another job somewhere," I replied but shud-
dered with revulsion inside at the idea of
going back to working for someone else.
But at least when I said that I knew that
entrepreneurship wasn't a one way ticket. I
had a technical skillset that was in demand.
I could get another job if it didn't workout.
(Fingers crossed that it would work out,
though.)*

I'm sure I am in good company with others making the
leap with thoughts like: "What if I can't make the money I
made in my old job? How will I pay the bills without putting
an extra burden on my husband?" "What if it's going really
well and suddenly, I have no clients or income?" I knew I

wouldn't be cut out for the business owner lifestyle if I had to live with fearful thoughts like these. So I called on my logic to come up with a strategy. Before I went down to part time in my job, I made sure I had my referral system lined up. I had already spoken to the cardiology practice and they were on board with recommending me to their patients. In addition to this, I had some clients who were becoming "regulars." When I felt confident that I had new business coming in, I would let go. I went part time over the holidays and in January went to working one day a week. Even though part of me just wanted to cut ties and break free, I knew that holding out for one more month was giving me that extra bit of a security blanket while my practice took shape. I picked up a handful of new clients rather effortlessly and realized, "this is it! this is how it happens, one client at a time." When I was finally on my own in February, I picked up another nine clients in addition to the diabetes class I taught. I had a feeling it was going to be ok and relaxed a bit.

To stay responsible, however, I did start tracking my numbers. In a notebook, I would track all of the income that came to me in the month. I would organize it by category, such as "insurance reimbursements, cash/ copays, Etsy sales, honey or other sales, and online business sales." Then every day that actual money was paid to me I would log it with the date and amount. This allowed me to see that in February, all sources of income (including the last few days of paid salary work) put me at about even with my typical take home pay. My eyes were in disbelief at what I was looking at. How did I manage to replace my income in my first month in business?

In actuality, I had been in business for a few months, I just didn't think of it as official because I still had a foot in my old job. Admittedly, gross income isn't quite the same as take home pay. I knew at some point I would have to be paying taxes on my income, but for now I wasn't feeling the pinch of less money. It was like magic! My new business was bringing in the same income I was earning from previous paychecks. I didn't realize this until the very end of the month when I actually tallied up the numbers. But there it was in black and white. And it kept growing into March and April as well. The great thing about the monthly income tally is that it allowed me to track my income over the year and look for patterns and fluctuations. It dipped in the summer time. My slowest month was July, but I also took a two week vacation that month. Then it started to ramp up again in August, September and October and slowed down through the holidays. I had to be fair and factor in vacation time. There is no "vacation pay" when you're self employed.

Overall, in my first year of self employment I grossed close to $50,000. About 90% of revenue was from the nutrition practice itself and 10% was from online endeavors and hobby business income. I was in total shock when I tallied up the numbers because it certainly didn't feel like I worked hard enough to earn that kind of money. In fact, there were a few moments when I decided to ease up on soliciting my services. After the puppy came along, much of my free time was spent outside with him and much less time was dedicated to self promotion or business development.

Lessons Learned:

- Before letting go of that full time job, I made sure I'd been working a couple of months part time, building up my clientele.

- When in doubt, I charted it out. I started making an excel spreadsheet or used pen and paper to really track revenue that was coming in. I added my totals week to week and evaluated at the end of each month.

- I set progress goals for myself- such as 10 new clients per month. I tracked everything. I was surprised how much money I really did have coming in and was be able to see which activities were worth spending more time on to reach my financial goals.

CHAPTER TEN

Dealing with Downers: Chasing Payments, No Shows, and Unsupportive Partnerships

"What do you mean I owe you money? My insurance didn't pay for it? You said it would be covered! I don't have the money to pay you anything. A hundred and forty dollars?! I need to see a bill for this." It was an actual conversation I was having with a client. "I know, I'm sorry, they explained it incorrectly to me. Apparently you have a deductible that hasn't been met yet. When I called and asked, they said the service would be covered. I can give you a self-pay discount and reduce the bill somewhat, but you will be getting a bill from me." It was the ugly part of the job. I hated telling patients that they owed me money after the fact, especially when they were under the impression that their insurance would cover everything. Most of the patients I saw didn't have the disposable income to see a nutritionist.

One of the unattractive sides to self employment is that I was personally responsible for my money. Sometimes this meant having to do a bunch of extra work to make it come to me. If my appointment didn't show, I didn't earn any money. If the insurance plan changed and the benefits dropped off, I didn't make money. The one nostalgia I had for my old job was when I used to get paid whether I counseled anybody or not. Paid time off was a nice benefit too! But now in my new realm of self employment, I had to deal the downers as well as the perks.

Getting paid. Normally, this was not an issue if the client had Blue Cross Blue Shield insurance. For the majority of plans, the Medical Nutrition Therapy benefit permitted 100% coverage, no copays or deductible. It made the process very smooth and easy, we never had to discuss money or payments. Occasionally, I would make an incorrect assumption and not make the phone call I need to make to verify benefits for some BCBS plans. It might turn out that there was a visit limit, or would only provide MNT for diabetes, or there was a high deductible or copay. Although this didn't happen very often, it made for a very uncomfortable and awkward situation when I had to call a client and inform them that their insurance didn't pay for their visit. This happened more frequently with Medicare plans like Humana, Blue Advantage and Coventry, where I was not in-network but would often get approved for payment on a special request. Typically these plans required pre-authorizations before rendering services, but I was not "in the know." I thought since I was a Medicare provider, I could see anyone who had a Medicare sponsored plan with the same guidelines. Live and learn. That's pretty much been my motto for the past year.

I ended up developing a better approach to unfamiliar insurance situations. Upfront, I let patients know that it's possible that their visit might not be covered. They would be responsible to pay for any portion that was not covered. I have them sign a statement stating this. Then, I call their company and verify the benefits. Lack of coverage isn't as much of a barrier as I thought it would be. Highly motivated patients are happy to pay cash for appointments, and I provide a courtesy discount for those patients who are self pay. I even provide an option for shorter 30 minute follow up appointments for those who need to budget more and this has worked out well. If I had to guess, I'd say that about 50% of people decline to schedule an appointment if they find out it won't be covered by insurance. If I was not taking insurance it would be much more challenging to work with the client demographic I see.

"No show" is my term for clients who schedule an appointment and then don't show up for it. Often this entails me driving to the office, only to wait around, call them at 15 minutes past the scheduled time to see if they might be lost and then realize I've wasted an hour of my day. Being a one woman show, I don't have time or energy to call and remind everyone about their upcoming appointments. I did develop an improved strategy to decrease my no shows. I realized that they tended to happen most frequently with new clients, people I hadn't established rapport or routine with yet. So for new clients, I would do a reminder call. Also, my scheduling software Dr Chrono provides a vigorous email reminder system. Amazingly, I do still have clients without email who tend to be elderly, so I prefer to reach out and call them, especially if it's a first time appointment. Some clients are a little scattered and need the reminder nudge, so I may send them an email, to see if "we're still on for Friday's appointment." A few clients prefer to text and that's a fairly easy way to send a reminder. For most clients, the automatic email reminders are enough and they usually email me to say if they need to reschedule.

I suppose the important thing to remember is that no shows and not getting paid are a normal part of business. Even hospital systems have to deal with these things. My no show rate is extremely low, less than 10 percent, and that's amazing when compared to my no show rate when I worked at the hospital where it was closer to 50%. Most of the time, clients just forgot their appointment. I know I've been on the other side of the fence before. It can feel challenging not to take it to heart.

I had great expectations for how things would work out in my business. The wellness center felt so right, but when the business didn't pick up, I had to realize that it was not the most supportive relationship to help my business grow. Likewise, I had to let go of the idea of working in the cardiology practice. I could have kept chasing it and "forced" the arrangement to work, but at what cost? Eventually the time investment and stress of uncertainty take its toll.

Again, it wasn't the fault of the cardiology practice, they were the ones who came to me initially. But other forces can come into play and change the winds of your business direction unexpectedly. This is what I had to prepare myself for as an entrepreneur. In the corporate world, change seems to happen at a snails pace- it drove me crazy! But in the entrepreneurial world, it was the exact opposite. One day might feel like being stuck in the mud, but in a moment, a new opportunity could pop out of the woodwork and re-energize my spirits. Riding out these waxing and waning currents without getting too caught up in the drama is a true skill.

Lessons Learned:

- Keep track of my payments. Inform clients ahead of time they may be liable for the balance of what insurance doesn't pay or if they deny the claim.

- One week I felt like nothing was going right and business my slipping from my fingers, however in a moment I could get a new referral, 3 new phone calls and payment on an outstanding claim. Learn to stay positive in between the ups and downs.

CHAPTER ELEVEN

Creating Products and Packages

"My goal for the end of the year is to complete my 30 day protocol program and offer it for sale to my newsletter list," I told my business coach. "And what do you need to do this week to make sure that happens?" she asked. "I need to spend two hours a day working on it. I need to write up my sales page. I need to highlight the benefits and features. I need to upload it onto the sales website. And I need to finish recording one of the videos." It seemed like a lot of work to do in 2 weeks. Technically I had all month to work on it, but I was going to be on Christmas vacation for two of them. To my delight, after getting all of my work done like a maniac, and getting the word out about my brand new program to all one hundred of my newsletter subscribers by mid-December, I actually had 3 sales of my Inflammation Free Zone 30 Day Protocol before the end of the month. I couldn't believe it! Did I just make money online, while I was on vacation? Was this the start of a new beginning?

Even before I opened my doors to my office, I had the idea that I wanted to have my own products that I could offer. The very first thing I created was a downloadable cookbook that I put together in PowerPoint. I made the recipes gluten free, dairy free, soy free and refined sugar free to appeal to those with food sensitivities. I also created a meal plan for the cookbook that included some seasonal variety. I added my own images and converted the entire file into a PDF document which I uploaded to my website. Additionally, I created some into DVDs and had these available for sale at promotional events. I also provided these resources to my clients at no cost.

It was a lot of work to compile all of the information and to format the design myself, but I was more concerned about having a final product available as a resource than I was with having a perfectly designed book. It was great having my own original resource to give to clients. It made me feel quite professional to say that I had my own cookbook that I created and that it also contained meal plans, it often saved me some work to help brainstorm menu ideas with clients. I also made it available for purchase on my website.

Then I had the idea that I wanted to create my own program, sort of like a 30 day protocol. I had purchased self guided protocols before from other respected health practitioners, so I had an idea of how to set up and execute a program like this. I knew that I needed to have a specific concept, which included an "approved" food list with some recipes and meal plan suggestions, as well as regular guidance. I decided on a 30 day "Inflammation Free" protocol and focused my suggested foods, recipes and supplements around this. All of this was on one big PDF document which was available for immediate download after purchase. Then, the other part of the program included other lifestyle interventions, such as stress management tips, toxin free cleaner and skin care recipes and weekly guided meditation. The program was delivered weekly via automated emails with videos from me and included a link to download the meditation for the week. It was a holistically designed program to help individuals reduce inflammation from diet and lifestyle. I called it "Inflammation Free Zone." I marketed it to my email list and had it available for sale on my website and was excited that it made a few sales before the end of the year which was my goal.

The product really came in handy later that spring. I came upon an opportunity to collaborate with a group of Paleo and Primal lifestyle enthusiasts to create a "product bundle." Basically, the "bundle" was a digital collection of cookbooks, meal plans, resource guides all geared towards the Paleo/Primal lifestyle. I offered to include my 30 day program as part of the bundle. Even though I was giving away my program, in exchange I would receive an affiliate bonus on every bundle sale I made personally. Even more importantly, my resource and my business would be getting a much broader exposure to a very large audience of individuals interested in nutrition. It was definitely a win-win situation. I added close to 800 new subscribers to my newsletter within a month from this project. That was quite a sizable jump in subscribers considering it took me two years to build my subscribership to over 200 members. I even gained a few clients from the exposure.

Lessons Learned:

- It was great to have my own program to recommend and a cookbook that I produced. I had the perfect outlet to promote my own products. Giving them freely to my clients increased my perceived value.

- Invite regular clients to any online or specialty programs I put on in addition to their one to one visits.

CHAPTER TWELVE

Mentoring and Precepting

"After finding your website, I read the story of how you began your business and how it also allows you the freedom to earn extra income
through your hobbies. It sounds so rewarding and is very inspiring to me! I also love your real food approach to nutrition and counseling.

I am currently working on my masters and dietetic internship. While I find the clinical realm of dietetics very interesting, I have always known that I wanted to work with people on a more personal level. I want to connect with patients and I want to see the long term results of my nutrition intervention. As of now, none of my rotations can provide me with that type of experience. I would really love to get some exposure in the private practice setting. I want to sharpen my counseling skills and observe how an experienced RD operates in a typical private nutrition counseling session. I am reaching out to you and wondering if you have ever worked with dietetic interns or if you might be interested in taking me on for a couple weeks of my community rotation.

I have spoken with my internship director about my desire to gain some experience in the private practice setting and she has communicated to me that it is possible if I can find an RD willing to take me on for a portion of my community rotation. I realize you are very busy, so if this is not possible I understand. Either way, I knew I wanted to reach out because I am so eager to learn about this career path in dietetics. Thank you so much for reading. I look forward to hearing from you."

My business model began to evolve over the course of the year. The more I figured out what I was doing, the more questions I could answer for others. This made me a valuable resource to other nutritionists with similar business aspirations. I've been contacted by students still in school or in their nutrition internships, looking for an RD to learn from or spend time with. I was able to accommodate them in a variety of ways. I did a couple of personal interviews and answered specific questions about working as a dietitian. One student intern came to see me in action doing a couple promotional events. I invited her to assist me during a health and wellness exposition. It was quite helpful to have her there to help answer questions, and it also provided her with the opportunity of what it was like to market one's services. Another student came to shadow me for a week in my office. She observed some consults with client permission and assisted me in creating a diabetes menu plan for a residential facility, which was great practice for her and great help for me as well. I did have the blessing and contract from the school internship director to make the opportunity sanctioned by the school. I had to review, sign and return a contract which stipulated the relationship I was to provide to the student. This is referred to as "precepting" a student intern.

I've also been a valuable resource to other nutritionists through private community groups on Facebook where I'm a member. Often, individuals will post questions about private practice, related to taking insurance or personal policies on operating a business. I usually have time to post a quick reply, just citing my experience, but even that periodic visibility as a business resource has paid off in spades. Sometimes these discussions continued as conversations offline in a private phone call. On a few occasions, I turned these conversations into an opportunity to ask the individual if they might be interested in working together. Not in a salesy kind of way, but I would more formally offer my "private nutrition business mentoring" to those who seemed most interested. Amazingly, many said "yes" to the offer.

Another way I've shared my knowledge and experience with nutrition professionals is by hosting webinars or online conferences. I've usually done these as a collaboration with other dietitian nutritionists so that we could share our collective wisdom on a particular topic. One webinar was done as a powerpoint presentation on the topic of "Starting a Private Practice." Other conferences were less formal and consisted of a video chat question and answer session, usually preceded a telling of my personal story. These are usually very well received and participants can get involved by asking direct questions to the presenters/hosts. It's also a great opportunity for increased exposure, by opening up the webinar or conference to anyone who may be interested in the topic. You can even use the webinar as an opportunity to promote a larger program, if you have more to offer on the topic. But it's equally as enjoyable to just share your experience with others who are curious about the process you've been through.

Another positive outcome of being able to share my experience and knowledge with other nutritionists is that it has helped to develop and strengthen my professional network. When I worked with individuals one on one, a more intimate relationship was created which built a greater trust. I went from being a unknown online personality to a trusted resource and friend to many.

Lessons Learned:

- Once I started figuring things out and start making things work for myself, others wanted to know how I did what I've done. Offering my services in the form of mentoring and or precepting students was another way to give back and share my wisdom with the nutrition community.

- The more I contributed, the more I became the "go-to" person for questions. This led to many other collaboration opportunities and side income in being a business coach and mentor to others.

CHAPTER THIRTEEN

Importance of Self Care Routines

Did I wear this outfit yesterday? Hmm. I couldn't be sure. I remember going out to get groceries in yoga pants, which also happen to be the pants I like to sleep in. I looked down at the sofa. Yup, the cushions are definitely warped with the impression of my rear end. I can't remember the last time I put on make up. Now that I think about it, I haven't been to the gym this week and it's Thursday. I really want to get my routine in order; I can't keep going like this. Right after I finish this blog post, I'm going to take the dog for a walk. Oh look, it's raining now. Well tomorrow then, I'm going to get back on track starting tomorrow!

The greatest learning curve for me at the start of my business had nothing to do with running my business. It was learning how to take care of myself while running a business. Even though self employment lends itself to flexible schedules and following the whim of your desire, the truth is that it's easy to forget about basic needs and self care.

At the beginning of my transition, I felt the need to be on task throughout the day, I had my days planned out to the hour and wanted to be as productive as possible in developing my business plans. However, what I came to realize is that I didn't leave much time for basic necessities such as taking a lunch break, going for a walk to clear my head and even time to prepare and fix dinner. I did become less driven over time and eventually was ok with getting a few key tasks or projects done in a day instead of tackling every item on my to do list.

I realized I needed to be more forgiving in my expectations of what I could get done in a day and what I was sacrificing to be so productive. Most of my business projects involved computer work and long hours typing and looking at the screen. This caused me to be much less active, with more time spent sitting at home on the couch. For a quick break, I would walk to the kitchen to grab a bite to eat and it wasn't long before these habits created a gradual pattern of weight gain.

Most of the time I spent working from home unless I had appointments scheduled. I would go into the office about 20 minutes before an appointment and might spend more time between clients working on daily tasks. For small activity breaks I would get up and mop the floor, do a load of laundry or do the dishes. It would be enough to give my brain a break and give my circulation a boost. One thing you'll hear from other people who work from home, and what started to bug me is that my environment didn't change much. For a person who loves variety, working in my living room in my pajamas actually got old. Sometimes if I didn't have to go into my office for a day or two and stayed at home working, I would start to feel as if the days were blending into one. I would get up, pull my hair back into a ponytail, work in my pajamas, tidy up the house, go to bed, and wake up again in the same outfit. I was beginning to wonder if I even needed all the clothes that were in my closet.

For me, working from home was not the most productive model. I would be distracted by house chores and my dog who needed constant attention. I knew that if I had a really important project that needed work, I would have to go to one of my offices and do the work there, undisturbed. It was just so tempting to not go into the office, because I didn't have to.

In the same vein, I found myself going to the late morning classes at the gym because I could. I would allow myself to sleep late because I no longer scheduled early morning appointments. But this also had its drawbacks. I would get back from the gym closer to 11 AM and suddenly after walking the dog and eating, my morning was gone. Morning is typically my most productive and focused time to get things done and the "flexibility" I was allowing myself was shooting me in the foot.

I did get back to a regular routine of exercise eventually. Having a flexible schedule may not have been the most productive for my business, but I think it contributed to my overall well-being. Since being self employed, I have not been sick at all. I generally get the sleep that I need and have the resources to make healthy meals most of the time. If I do feel something coming on, I am able to back off of some responsibilities, take it easy, get more rest and keep the stress at bay. It may also be influenced by the fact that I'm happier and my immune system is robust, or that I'm exposed to much fewer sick people. Whatever the reason, I'm sure it's a combination of factors that have kept me healthy over the past year or so.

Lessons Learned:

- I gained 10 pounds in my first year of business working for myself mostly due to more frequent seated computer work as well as a lack of attention on exercise and eating routines. Working from home more often meant more opportunity to snack while taking a break.

- Having my own business can be stressful and have it's share of ups and downs. Following a good routine of self care including healthy foods, adequate exercise, stretch breaks, plenty of sleep helped me cope with the stress much easier.

CHAPTER FOURTEEN

Failed Ideas

Everyone was looking at me with respectful attention as I gave my weekly update. And then, I broke into tears. "I just worked so hard and developed this program and nobody is interested! Only one person signed up for the webinar and then nobody showed up on the day of the presentation. Only one person was interested in the mentoring program, and you can't run a program with just one person. And now I had all of these people who were supposedly so interested in my weight loss retreat, but when I called them to confirm, they all either changed their minds or had to back out at the last minute. What am I doing wrong?!" My voice was shaky as I let out my frustration. The women in my business mastermind group were quietly watching me come undone, but I could feel their empathy. They knew how hard I'd been working the past few months to create and launch a successful program.

In the course of figuring out my business and what I wanted to offer to the world, like most entrepreneurs, I found out that not every idea I had was popular. My very first creation was downloadable cookbook, which probably could have been designed better but was a solid resource for clients. I created a contest on Facebook to raffle off three copies of the cookbook and this generated lots of interest. I gained about a dozen newsletter subscribers from this strategy and awarded a free consult as a top prize for sharing the contest. Despite the initial interest in my cookbook, the funny things is that I have never sold a copy from my website. Does that make the cookbook a failure? No, but it doesn't seem to be the "must have" resource that people are looking for when they are browsing my website.

The next thing I created was a holiday weight management program. I created an online course, which was quite an ambitious endeavor and marketed it to my newsletter. I enticed people with a free guide to lose belly fat as a free gift for joining the program. I had about ten people sign up which was really exciting. I would send communications to the enrollees before the course launch, prepping them for the start of the program. I eagerly created all of the course content in the meantime. I advertised on my Facebook page and in my community groups. When the first class started, I had one person join in. I was so confused. Where were the other 8 people who signed up? I wondered. Do I continue to offer the course next week with just one person? Turns out, the following week, that one person didn't show up either. Rah! I was livid. All of this work I had put into the course and nobody followed through with the class. I knew I had missed something along the way, but I was still trying to figure all of this out. I knew my content was good. I had led similar programs for worksite wellness in previous job and people loved it! I figured that I would need to do a post-mortem analysis of sorts to really figure out why I didn't have the participants like I thought I would. Turns out, most people just wanted the free belly fat guide and missed the rest of my communication emails.

I wasn't deterred from creating programs however. I knew that if I could create a quality program, I could make it my signature program. I could continue refine it and offer it consistently. I thought about what was popular in the nutrition scene at the time. It seemed that DIY 30 Day Programs were getting a lot of attention, so I set off to create one of my own. I decided on an anti-inflammation program and added more content that went beyond nutrition. My intention was to create a holistic program that also addressed lifestyle and environment and daily habits. The Inflammation Free Zone was created! Between a PDF resource and weekly emails, recipes and recorded meditations and videos, it was one of the most comprehensive resources I had put together. I had a pretty good response when I shared it with my newsletter subscribers and it turned out to be the perfect resource to share the following year as part of a e-book bundle. Although the program hasn't generated many sales on its own, I think of it as a success because of how much it has been shared and used. It's very possible that I could do more promoting and targeted marketing, possibly other collaborations to help make the program more popular.

In January of 2014, I partnered up with a colleague to promote a webinar on starting a successful nutrition practice. We had quite a bit of interest and sign ups for the webinar and had lots of interaction while doing the presentation. At the end of the webinar, we announced our ten week Nutrition Business Mentoring program that we would be launching in the spring. We created an application process for individual who were interested in learning more about the program. At the end of the webinar, an email was sent out to the participants with a copy of the Mentorship program application. There were eight weeks of curriculum and open office calls on the other two weeks. Participants also had access to both instructors for private one to one coaching. It was a robust program with lots of value and we priced it at $997. Despite the interest and activity during the webinar, we received only one application back out of all 22 participants. It was a huge blow for us, as we were quite excited to shift into a new role as mentors and get started on creating all of the course content. I tried not to read too much into it, but it seemed like a trend. Just one person interested. I guess that's better than zero interest. But it had us going back to the drawing board.

My colleague and I loved the idea of collaborating together to offer online programs. We lived in different states and it was a fun way for us to stay in touch and work together. Our next thought was to broaden our reach to a larger demographic. We both had newsletter lists filled with people interested in healthy eating, many who were also concerned with weight loss. We thought that perhaps we didn't reach a large enough demographic with our business webinar, so we would try again with a new program where we could broaden our marketing. We got started on the initial webinar titled "4 Ways to Lose Weight without Dieting Anymore." At the end of the webinar we announced our new online program called "Weight Loss Pleasure Camp." Both of us felt this was the right move, to appeal to our current clients and subscribers. We marketed the webinar on all of our online platforms, LinkedIn, Facebook (I even created a Facebook Ad), newsletters and Twitter. We were noticing that our sign ups weren't robust, so we pushed our webinar date out a couple of weeks to see if we could rally up more interest. When the day came for our webinar, we didn't know what to expect, and it turned out that we had just one person show up for the webinar. We were floored and completely taken by surprise by the lack of interest in our program. We both knew from personal experience that people LOVED learning about non-diet approaches for weight loss. We knew that people NEEDED to learn about alternatives to dieting. But why the lack of participation? After hearing from other entrepreneurs, it turns out that intense marketing and large numbers are likely the biggest factors in determining ultimate participation.

There really was no way of knowing for sure what we could have done better but it sure had my entrepreneurial spirit in the dumps. It felt as though I had been trying so hard all year creating programs yet no one seemed inter-ested enough to participate. I was sick of it. Despite the support of my lovely colleague, I suddenly lost interest in developing and marketing online programs.

Lessons Learned:

- Don't be afraid to let go of ideas that aren't working out even if I've spent a lot of time working on them. Sometimes "forcing" something to happen is a sign that it's not meant to be.

- Check in and re-evaluate how excited I am about an idea. I was surprised to find my own interests ebb and flow and needed to allow myself to move on while leaving a previous idea behind.

- Ask for feedback. Did I get enough input before I de-veloped my idea? Is my subject relevant and in high demand? Did people see or hear my message?

- It's easy to look at what's failing, however, also take inventory of what is working. Perhaps I could redi-rect my energy into areas that are working well to make those even better.

CHAPTER FIFTEEN

Definition of Success

Here I am taking night classes, but there's no dreaded studying involved. I'm elated to be here. I look up at the building and the lighted sign that reads "Sawtooth School of the Arts." I'm taking a class in enameling jewelry. It's the fourth class I've taken this year at the school and it's really put me back in my creative element. I have that sense of what it felt like to be ten years old and so focused on a project that I lose track of time. It's incredible! The designs I am creating are coming out perfectly as though I've been doing this all of my life, except that it was my first time attempting to enamel copper. I texted my friend after class. "My 3 hour class felt like 20 minutes. My bliss exploded. I made the best project tonight! It's like I can feel the divine speaking to me and its voice is the giddiness and elation I feel…" I was doing exactly what made me happy and I was so grateful to have the time and the money to invest in activities I valued.

At the beginning of my new business journey, I was using income as my primary metric for success. As long as I was making enough money to pay the bills, I knew I was "making it." When I saw I was making the same money from my previous job I felt like I was "killing it." Then when business dipped in the summer and over the holidays, I started to doubt if I was truly successful. Maybe I was fooling myself that I was going to make more money than I ever had before.

Once I noticed this mindset of "lack" starting to raise its ugly head, I realized I needed to step back and reframe my perspective. I could pay the bills. I had more time on my hands to spend developing my online business. I had spare time to take jewelry classes at the art school. I had time to work on making jewelry for craft shows and participate in them. I could be fully attentive to my honeybees. I had the leisure time to spend with my puppy at the dog park or hiking in the woods. I spent more time with my stepchildren when they were visiting over the summer. I had flexibility in my schedule to take a vacation any time I wanted for as long as I wanted without advanced notice. If this wasn't success, what was?

I became more forgiving and trusting of the ebb and flow of income throughout the year and gave myself permission to "take it easy" when things were slow. The nature of being self employed is that you will have times where business is booming, you are super busy and have little downtime, as well as times where things are quite sluggish, things fall apart or don't work out and you have more free time at your leisure. By embracing the flow, I could knuckle down and work really hard when I had to, because I knew it wasn't a permanent mode of operation. Likewise, when things were more slow paced, they happened to coincide with summer vacations, holidays or bad weather and it gave me a reprieve to enjoy downtime for myself at the same time. It was nice to find out clients weren't demanding appointments over the Christmas break, so I didn't feel so bad about taking a two week vacation during that time.

I could have taken a different approach and stayed busy with business development during my practice downtime. In fact, this is what I did in the first few months of my new business. I wasn't as busy day to day with clients, so I really focused on creating and marketing online programs. I could have spent every free moment trying to further my business, but for what reasons? It was just as summer was starting when I decided to take a different approach to downtime. Instead of keeping myself bogged down with projects, I languished in the slower pace. I gave myself permission to enjoy the fruits of my labor. I had been working so hard all year and things were going well, so why not push less and enjoy more?

One day I was trying to multitask and thought I could bring my laptop with me to the lake where I walk my dog. I let him play in the water and I sat down in a folding canvas chair. I plopped myself on the ground with my laptop and looked out at the water, watching my dog's delight as he fetched logs. In that moment, I realized I had fulfilled a vision I had for myself from many years ago. I had wanted to be able to work from anywhere, sit outside, work on my computer and be completely surrounded by nature. It struck me that I had achieved the vision I saw for my ideal career! Sure, it was a little less glamorous than the glossy magazine image I had glued to my vision board. There were more dirt and distractions in nature. But the feeling was still there. It was like magic. An idea had come to life that was at one point just a dream of mine.

Lessons Learned:

- When I realized I had more time for hobbies that were important to me, making more money didn't matter as much. I felt like I had already achieved the outcome that money would buy me.

- There are many ways to make a good living while in business for myself, it just depended on how I want to spend my time. If my main focus is creating income, I could choose to spend downtime creating more programs or developing an online presence. I am allowed to decide what my definition of success is.

CHAPTER SIXTEEN

Highlights From My First Year

I can't believe that all of this has happened. I still can't believe I'm not working in my old job. I can't believe that my one hour commute has just disappeared! I can't believe that all I have to carry to work is my ipad. I'm amazing that I can talk to clients one day and get paid 2 weeks later in my bank account. I can't believe how easy this is. I need to write a book about this. I had to figure all of this out for myself. I had no idea where to start, but just kept asking questions wherever I could and now look at me. I'm actually self employed. I never thought this was possible for me! And here I am a year later. It's still working and getting better all the time. The funny part is that I can't believe that I started out just trying to start a website and ended up with a full fledged private practice with two office locations and contracted with insurance companies. My, my how the tide has changed!

So much can happen in the course of a year. Anyone who's been married or had a baby can relate to this. The same goes for the beginnings of a new business. It starts as a twinkle in your eye, then the seed starts to grow. Suddenly 9 months later (plus or minus) I was faced with an entirely new reality. I gave birth to a business baby. When I first started my business journey, it felt more like an exploration or a hobby. I had no intentions of leaving my job in less than a year. I had no idea where the road was going to take me. All I knew was that I kept taking action steps in the direction I wanted to head.

I stayed conservative. I didn't spend tons of money. I kept my full time job until I saw the new money coming in. I made lots of connections and grew my networking community. I learned from others but also taught myself how to design my website and make products and programs. When I had more money, I invested it back into my business and upgraded my website and my laptop. I kept track of my expenses and hired an accountant at the end of the year to help me figure out my taxes. I made easy money. I put money aside. I worked long days. I worked for free. I spent hours and hours in front of a computer. I made money I didn't expect to. I volunteered my time. I had insurance claims that didn't get paid. I worked when I needed to and was paid "per job" instead of "hourly."

Summing up my year, I highlighted the things that just made me giddy with excitement or proud as a peacock. These were my favorite moments:

1. Leaving my old job. no more long distance commutes, out of town travelling, 9 to 5 days or boring office meetings and mandatory trainings

2. Collaboration with the pharmacy that allowed for independence, an office space just outside of town and a steady referral stream of patients

3. Creation and promotion of my own anti-inflammation 30 day program

4. Meeting and working with a group of like-minded business women for ongoing support

5. Connecting and contributing to an online community of like-minded nutritionists

6. Being able to afford custom logo branding and upgraded website design

7. Offering mentoring as a service to other RDs

8. Having time for hobbies that brought in supportive income streams

9. Writing a book about my hobby crafts and sold on Amazon

10. Having took 3 vacations that were 1-2 weeks long

11. Getting a puppy and had time to care for him

12. Making nearly $50,000 working part time (seeing clients than 15 hours a week)

Despite having these "big wins" throughout the year, I'm most proud of the fact that I followed through on my desire to create a business for myself. I had a particular plan in mind at the beginning, but I stayed true to myself when I realized that I wanted something more. I knew I could have kept my old job, gradually built an online business and skipped the whole private practice thing, but it wouldn't have resonated with my deepest values of independence, creativity, self-reliance and adventure. Yes, adventure is important to me. Taking a risk and trying something new is how I want to live my life, career included. The bonus gift came in learning who I was as an entrepreneur. Reflecting on my resourcefulness, self-reliance and resilience has given me a new appreciation and confidence in myself. I know that I can do anything I set my mind to, even if it doesn't turn out exactly picture perfect. Seeing myself through a new lens, with a new identity, I almost can't believe all that I've accomplished in one year. Being able to appreciate all of it and have gratitude for the blessings of support that have come my way is truly how I want to embrace and celebrate my first year in business.

CHAPTER SEVENTEEN

Goals for my next year

Ugh. I can't believe all this money is going to taxes. I had been putting aside a little bit of money throughout the year because I knew I would have to pay my share at the end fo the year. I had a lot of expenses and deductions, but I was also making pretty good money and that meant you have pay Uncle Sam come tax time. But, what the heck? I don't understand these tax work-sheets. I texted my sister, who happens to be an accountant. "So will I be faced with a penalty if I've not been paying quarter-ly estimates all year?" She pops in a quick reply "No, you can pay it all in a lump sum. Plus Bryan has been paying taxes all year, so you should be fine." But I wasn't sure if I could count on that. I was planning to file separately because the business stuff was so confusing. I didn't want to muddle up the filing. I calculated numbers. I processed the worksheets. I didn't like what I was com-ing up with. "What is this self-employment tax? It's practically doubling what I owe!" I screamed with frustration. I put the paper-work down. I had to not think about this for

*a little while. A few weeks later, I was look-
ing for an accountant to take over all of this
for me. There's a time for DIY and there's
a time to hire a professional. The time had
come to call in a pro. It was the best $300
I'd spent all year.*

In the midst of running my business, I found myself constantly making decisions that weren't always based on
experience. Sometimes I just had to wing it, and I was ok
with that. My attitude was "that's how you learn." There's
a learning curve to everything. By the end of the year I
was able to gain much more insight on how these decisions affected me by looking at everything from a broader
perspective. Then, I took this information and made better
decisions going forward. These are the top areas I chose
to focus on improving for business year #2.

Better Record Keeping

In retrospect, I was quite proud and amazed how things
turned out in my first year. Some of it was good planning,
some was just luck and some events served as true teaching moments.

Probably the most notable area where I could improve
in my business was in my record keeping. I had an easy
way to track my visits through my EMR software, but I
needed better organization in tracking my expenses. I did
use the app Evernote to track my expenses, but incon-
sistently. Evernote has the functionality to help you tag
emails, photos, web pages, even screenshots to capture

notes on anything you may need to keep a tally on. It's a tool with great potential and I hope to make better use of it in the future. There were still gaps and missing data though. Luckily most everything is trackable online either through email, bank accounts or Amazon order history. I was able to hunt down all of my expenses purchased on-line, but it sure took up a lot of time that could have been better spent doing more productive tasks. I needed a more consistent and efficient tracking system that would have all of my information organized by category and tallied at the end of the year. With a little more practice I felt I could optimize using Evernote for this purpose. It would just re-quire mindful diligence to track my expenses. Additionally, my accountant recommended using Quickbooks to keep track of income and expenses. Apparently the program has many other capabilities as well, which I am just start-ing to look into.

Improved Collaborations

As much as I was helped by having a cardiology prac-tice and the pharmacy diabetes program funnel referrals to me, I still felt like I could have made greater strides in growing my community network by seeking out key col-laborations. As it turned out in January of 2015, I was ap-proached by the owner of my gym who asked if I would be interested in offering my nutrition services to members. It was a perfect opportunity, I was already at the gym quite frequently and was familiar with the trainers and the members there. We worked out an arrangement where I would teach some workshops in exchange for use of office space to see clients. Periodically I would provide special discounts to new members. Within a week I had created a Nutrition Services flyer with my picture on it and had it posted around the fitness center. I also connected with a local manager at GNC to do some promotions in his store. Answering questions for customers while increasing my visibility was another way I was willing to spend a few hours of downtime marketing myself in a fun environment.

The other way I hope to collaborate with other health professionals is to expand my contributions and presence in the online world. I was fortunate in my first year to get connected to a prominent Paleo/Primal nutrition group that puts together a robust, annual resource bundle that reaches a very large audience. I had quite a large boost in visibility from this collaboration and plan to seek out and be available for other similar opportunities. I knew that there could be quite a bit of potential to expand my online networking community if I were to focus on consistently contributing and collaborating with other online health professionals.

Better Daily Routines

When I worked full time and had the most demanding schedule, I was a master at time management. It's a little ironic. It seems like the opposite would be true, that the less free time I had, the harder it would be to have everything fit into a daily schedule. The reality is that the less "free time" I had, the fewer options I had about where I could fit things into my schedule. The fewer options I had, the fewer decisions I had to make. The fewer decisions I had to make, the less mentally draining it was. It was as simple as deciding between now or never. There was only one option to workout at the gym (early morning at 6am). There was only one option for healthy breakfast and lunch (that I bring my pre-made meals to work with me.) There was one option for cleaning the house (on weekends.)

When I compared this to having a schedule that is completely flexible 80 percent of the time, the decision of where to fit things was not so straightforward. If I wasn't scheduling things based on the only option I had, I was tempted to do things when I "felt like it" or when I "had time later." There never seemed to be the threat of running out of time, so things easily got postponed. This was applicable in a variety of scenarios: working on a project, writing a book, going to the gym or getting the groceries. The danger in having a flexible schedule is that I got out of the habit of creating routines for myself. When I fell out of routine, it was much harder to sustain good habits.

Multiple Income Streams

As much as I've mentioned generating income my hobby business: crafts and jewelry, my nutrition practice was still my cash cow in terms of generating income. About 94% of my income came from one to one consults. About 2% came from group nutrition workshops. Another 2% came from the Etsy store and craft show income from my hobby business. And the other 1-2% came from online affiliate programs, mentoring, book royalties, and online consults. Technically I already had multiple income streams, but I wanted to spread the wealth more equally. I wanted to grow the rest of my arms of my business and generate more income in the other areas. Over time, this would get me to be less dependent on having the private practice as my primary income stream.

It makes good business sense to have income come from multiple areas. If one area isn't going so great, you can be supported by the other areas. I noticed happen on a small scale during the month of December when nutrition consults were slow, and vacation took up half the month. However, due to a craft show and holiday shopping in my Etsy store, I was able to compensate some income with my hobby.

I would like to generate more passive income streams by writing more books, guides and creating self led programs. I have the idea to create some online courses as well, but I want to really have my niche clearly defined and have done some preliminary marketing to assess the demand before I expend the effort to create another course. I also plan to include key affiliate programs (such as the Breezing Metabolism Tracker) and partnerships in my website and recommendations.

CHAPTER EIGHTEEN

The Long Term Vision

I'm in a tiny house on a mountain top in Colorado. Its not much bigger than 400 square feet, which is amusing considering I grew up in a house close to 4000 square feet. However, I'm not living here by mistake. It's an intentional decision. The goal was to simplify, to get down to bare essentials in order to live within our means. Achieving the "American Dream" to me and my husband is not about spending more and having more. For us, it's about being able to put our hand-crafted mark on our lifestyle. We are not willing to accrue more debt in order to build a dream house. We will earn it through a labor of love. We will not be in a place where we need to 'make a living' just to pay off a mortgage. We work because we choose to. We spend our time how we want to. We live sustainably. We live joyfully. We live happily ever after.

Ultimately, what appeals to me as an entrepreneur is to be able to have the freedom to pursue the lifestyle that makes me happy. I originally started my nutrition business journey with the intention of having an web based practice that would allow me to be location independent. This way, my husband and I could move to the mountains and I would be able to work from home. Instead, I opened up a local practice that enabled me to work less and develop other areas of my life, including hobbies that generate income as well. By allowing myself to spend more time on making jewelry, writing and creating art, I've decided that these interests are more meaningful and fulfilling to me than the desire to continue to pursue and develop a nutrition based business.

It's a little unsettling to think of myself not working as a registered dietitian. After all, I went to school for 7 years, obtained two degrees, acquired specialty certifications, and racked up some decent student loan debt. I'm not sure I'm ready for it to be "over" just yet. But that's ok. I don't have to know the answer to this now. The beauty about the job market in this day and age is that it's a creative economy. I can make money online and in other avenues instead of choosing the 9 to 5 career path.

In the long term, I don't see myself with a local nutrition practice. I don't see myself working with insurance companies. I may be still advising a few clients on nutrition, but this would be in an online capacity only. I may be mentoring other RDs in how to get their local businesses started. I may be doing some web based health coaching as an independent contractor. This may be what pays the bills for awhile and allows me flexibility to work from home so that I may still be location independent. I may be partnering with other health professionals online to contribute my unique message about life balance, fulfillment and happiness. I plan to diversify my income in many areas, so that I can be supported even if one area is not doing well.

I will continue to be engaged in my creative pursuits. I will likely create more bee themed hobbies. I may choose to write another book, perhaps focused on bees or on crafting the lifestyle of my dreams. I may be inclined to develop some creative retreats for people seeking to escape the 9 to 5 lifestyle and instead design a simpler, more sustainable life. I know I will be getting my hands dirty. I know I won't be in a cubicle. I know I can't be certain what will happen, but I do know that key opportunities will show up at the right time to support me following my dream.

My husband and I plan to move to the mountains of Colorado in a way that will not put us further into debt. We plan to pay off our student loans before we move. We plan to build a tiny home so that we can build it for cash and live in it while we build our dream home. We will be living more sustainably. I won't have the pressure to find a "full time job" because our expenses will be greatly reduced from what they are now. My best ideas have yet to come to me. I trust in the creative process because it hasn't let me down yet.

CHAPTER NINETEEN

Timeline of my First Year in Business

Although I consider the "official" start date of my business year to be January of 2014, it's important to note that I'd been taking action on the idea for about 9 months before that while I was still employed in my other job. This timeline starts back at my first intention to begin the journey towards self employment listing the actions taken prior to me quitting my job and being on my own.

March 2013: Enrolled in B-School to learn about starting a business online. Began working on developing a website, a company brand and wrote articles for my newsletter.

April 2013: Attended a Health and Wellness conference and networked with local Health practitioners to put myself out there as a nutrition professional

May 2013: Worked on creating a cookbook and seasonal meal plan to sell on my website, continued writing articles for my website and sending monthly newsletters to subscribers

June 2013: Followed up with potential business partners from the health fair. Researched dietitians in private practice in North Carolina.

July 2013: Finished my cookbook and created a downloadable e-book. Looked into contracting with insurance companies and began the credentialing process with accrediting agencies.

August 2013: Signed a 6 month lease with a business associate in order to have my own office space to practice. Gave advance notice to my manager at my current job that I intended to leave by the end of the year.

September 2013: Spent more time marketing business including a grand opening at the Wellness Center, evening and weekend nutrition classes to patrons of the Wellness Center.

October 2013: Became contracted with Blue Cross Blue Shield as an In-Network provider. Met with the head of a cardiology practice to discuss the idea for an in-house dietitian arrangement on a part time basis to be the preferred RD for referrals.

November 2013: Saw and billed my first client with insurance and received my first reimbursement check from Blue Cross Blue Shield. Became contracted with Medicare. Went down to part time status at my salaried job.

December 2013: Saw my first Medicare client. Had my first follow up appointment with a client. Finished my unique 30 Day program: Inflammation Free Zone and made a few sales among my newsletter subscribers. Took a 2 week vacation over Christmas.

January 2014: My last month at my salaried job working just 1 day per week. Picked up several new clients. Partnered with a pharmacy to teach diabetes classes in exchange for referrals. Held a webinar on starting a private practice with RD colleague. Developed the structure and content for a Nutrition Business Mentorship 10 week program.

February 2014: Learned the Wellness center was closing and moved office location into the pharmacy next door. Followed up with Nutrition Business Mentorship prospects, made offers to mentor individually. Took an online course in marketing high end programs and services.

March 2014: My busiest month of the year so far. Collaborated with RD colleague to launch an online weight management program. Hosted a book club meeting on The Desire Map and made some key connections. Continued marketing myself as a Nutrition Business Mentor.

April 2014: My highest revenue month of the year so far. Opened up a second office in town inside of a chiropractic facility. Began a local business Mastermind group for monthly support and feedback. Marketed my business at local Health and Wellness Expo. Developed concept and marketed programs for non-diet weight loss programs. Applied for network contract with Aetna.

May 2014: Wrote an e-book on my hobby business with crafts and beekeeping, published to Amazon Kindle library. Took a step back from creating online programs and products. Got a new German Shepherd puppy. Hired a web design company to redesign my logo, brand and website.

June 2014: Launched new website. Spent more time with new puppy and visiting step-children enjoying the summer. Picked up a nutrition business mentoring client. Created a new summer meals cookbook for website.

July 2014: Took a two week vacation to Vermont. Spent more time on hobbies. Confirmed in-network contract with Aetna.

August 2014: Held a large group nutrition workshop for a company and grossed $1500 in a day. Business began to pick back up. Took a 1 week vacation in Colorado.

September 2014: Busiest month of the year.

October 2014: Biggest revenue month of the year. Picked up a new nutrition business mentoring client. Precepted a nutrition intern student for a week. Purchased a new laptop.

November 2014: Started calculating estimated taxes to be paid. Created a new cookbook compilation for website opt-in gift.

December 2014: Took a two week vacation over Christmas. Slowest month of the year, after getting started in January. Highest revenue month for arts/crafts/hobby business.

January 2015: Paid in estimated taxes to IRS for 2014 in a lump sum. Purchased new indirect calorimeter device. Established a new partnership with my gym where I would eventually move my local office location. Met with tax accountant to discuss best approach for filing.

CHAPTER TWENTY

Parting Words of Wisdom

If you have the burning desire to start a nutrition business of your own, I encourage you to take those thoughts seriously by taking action. Taking action doesn't imply that you need to take drastic action, either. With a couple of hours a day you can do some research in your local area, network and make community connections, start a blog, begin designing a nutrition program or simply brainstorm ideas and put them into a vision board. Small daily actions over time will create huge results by generating momentum and sustaining consistent focus on developing your business. Start talking to people about your idea and see how that energizes you. If you get more and more excited the more you work on it, then you know you are on the right path.

If you ignore the feeling, it may come back to haunt you. You might find yourself unsatisfied in your work, bored in a particular career role or even find yourself job hopping every few years. However, not everyone is suited for the lifestyle of self employment. The entrepreneurial spirit has unique character. You need to be able to withstand some unpredictable fluctuations. You'll need to take risks. You'll need to be adventurous. You'll need to be unafraid to fail. You'll need resilience to pick yourself up from failure and keep going. You'll need to be resourceful. You'll need to reach out for support. You'll need to get out side of your comfort zone more than you'd like. You'll need to experiment and let go of expectations. You'll need to trust that the next step will appear if you make the first move.

For myself, I can identify a few key circumstances that allowed my business to be as successful as it was in its first year. Not everyone will have the same set of circumstances, so I caution using my story as an exact formula to replicate your business success. Firstly, I've been a registered dietitian for over 10 years. This experience has provided me with a huge amount of confidence in myself and abilities. I have learned specific skills, been trained in diabetes management, and this has likely helped boost my credibility as a nutrition professional, possibly making me more desirable to partner with.

I'm also quite comfortable talking about my strengths, skills and experience as an RD. When I spoke with the pharmacy and cardiology practice, my professionalism was evident which likely made it easier for the interested parties to make the decision to collaborate with me. I'm not sure that I could have exhibited this type of confidence and professionalism if I was new in my career. If you are just starting out, I recommend finding a way to develop your voice and boost your confidence so that you can stand out as a strong and knowledgeable professional. This could be something like teaching workshops or classes at the local health food store. As a new graduate it's hard to keep that in mind that you probably more about nutrition than most other people, including health professionals in other disciplines.

Another thing that made this transition easier for me was that I had a life partner to support me through my transition. Being married gave me confidence to take a few risks that I may not have considered otherwise. In the back of my mind, I knew I had a bit of a safety net just in case I didn't make a lot of money my first few months. We had some savings between the two of us, so knowing that, it helped me rationalize taking risks. Remarkably, I barely had to touch our savings. I was still able to pay the bills, the mortgage, and get groceries from my own bank account with money that I had earned.

I also had the option to go onto my husband's health insurance plan. Nowadays, if you're self employed, you need to have proof of health insurance when it comes tax time or you'll face a penalty. The fact that he had a health plan I could join made this much less stressful. I didn't have to worry about an additional monthly expense of health insurance premiums. You don't need to be married to have a financial safety net. You can create your own by saving up some money, perhaps 3 to 6 months of living expenses as you make your transition into self employment.

My husband was also a key liaison to networking with the cardiology practice. I had an advantage in that I had already met several of the partners of the practice and they were happy to refer patients to me. This built-in connection saved me some work on the ground. I didn't have to do the work to create this relationship. I also had the good fortune of being recommended to the pharmacy. I'm not sure I would call it a personal advantage, but the partnership was certainly instrumental in helping me broaden my practice and expand my reach into neighboring towns. Take an inventory and reach out to your social network. You never know who your friends and acquaintances may be able to connect you to.

The other key piece that allowed my nutrition practice to be financially successful was the ability to contract with insurance companies and market my services to clients with insurance. Even though I only initially contracted with two companies, the population in my area was large enough that there was no shortage of potential clients. In my local area, the benefit plans for nutrition were quite generous and allowed for multiple visits throughout the year. This helped me to create long lasting relationships with clients without the burden of addressing financial barriers of the client.

I'm certain that my local practice would have been more difficult to sustain had I not become a contracted provider. Financial barriers are frequently cited as the primary reason people choose not to work with me. The generous reimbursement from insurance companies enabled me to see fewer clients and work less hours in the office. I didn't have to worry myself about meeting quotas or selling nutrition packages. I'm not saying that you can't build a successful business with a cash based practice. In fact, most of the nutritionists I know in private practice have cash only practices and many of them work online as well. Personally, however, I feel my local practice took off the way it did because of my ability to bill insurance for services and that in my area, most people have insurance plans that provide great nutrition benefits. If you're considering working with insurance companies as part of your business model, I highly encourage you to speak with other dietitians in your state and local areas to research the viability of this option.

If you live in a smaller, more rural area, this option may not be viable. You may not have the population density to generate spontaneous referrals from the insurance network. It all depends on how you are getting your referrals. If you are connected to a busy practice or fitness center who eagerly refers their patients for nutrition services, you may be in luck!

Ultimately, I am so grateful for the opportunity I gave myself by deciding to pursue self employment by opening my own nutrition practice. If anyone were to ask me my regrets, I regret that I didn't pursue this opportunity sooner. I didn't realize that it was available to me. I didn't realize how sustainable it was. I didn't realize how quickly it could happen. I didn't realize I had it in me. The grit, the persistence and determination to "figure out" how to have my own nutrition business have carried me through periods of self doubt. Looking back on the past year and half, I couldn't be more satisfied with the way things turned out. It's been a journey of self discovery that has led to a new appreciation of self efficacy. I can now say that I've achieved a personal and professional goal that I've wanted for a long time, to be able to say I have my very own business and have even written a book about it.

40218733R00080

Made in the USA
San Bernardino, CA
13 October 2016